DATE DUE

The Century

for Young People

For a complete overview of the most eventful
hundred years in human history, you'll want to read these
companion volumes:

The Century for Young People:
Becoming Modern America: 1901–1936

The Century for Young People:
Changing America: 1961–1999

PETER JENNINGS
TODD BREWSTER

Adapted by Jennifer Armstrong

The Century
for Young People

Defining America
1936–1961

DELACORTE PRESS

This is the second volume of a three-volume adaptation of *The Century for
Young People*, by Peter Jennings and Todd Brewster. Based upon the work
The Century, by Peter Jennings and Todd Brewster, published by Doubleday
Books, a division of Random House, Inc., New York, in 1998.

Visit us on the Web! www.randomhouse.com/teens

Educators and librarians, for a variety of teaching tools, visit us at
www.randomhouse.com/teachers

Library of Congress Cataloging-in-Publication Data
Armstrong, Jennifer.
The century for young people / Peter Jennings, Todd Brewster ; adapted
by Jennifer Armstrong. — 1st trade pbk. ed.
p. cm.
Includes index.
ISBN 978-0-385-73768-5 (v. 1 : trade pbk.) — ISBN 978-0-385-90681-4
(v. 1 : glb) — ISBN 978-0-375-89396-4 (e-book) 1. History, Modern—20th
century—Juvenile literature. 2. History, Modern—20th century—Pictorial
works. I. Jennings, Peter, 1938–2005. Century. II. Brewster, Todd. Century.
III. Title.
D422.A76 2009
909.82—dc22
2009008437

The text of this book is set in 12-point Sabon.
Printed in the United States of America
10 9 8 7 6 5 4 3 2 1
First Trade Paperback Edition

For our children:
Elizabeth, Christopher, and Jack

CONTENTS

Introduction *ix*

1. Over the Edge 1936–1941 *1*

2. Global Nightmare 1941–1945 *33*

3. An Uneasy Peace 1946–1952 *60*

4. Mass Markets 1953–1961 *83*

Index *109*

INTRODUCTION

If you are one of those people who consider history to be the study of dry and boring facts, please think again. You are in for a surprise when you read these books. Well-told history is as compelling as any great novel or movie. It is full of drama, tension, interesting characters, and fantastic events. That is what you will find here, in this, the history—or should we simply say "story"?—of the twentieth century.

One hundred years may seem like a long time ago, but actually, this is fairly recent history. It is really not too far removed from your life today—and the story of the twentieth century is not just any old story. It is the story of your parents and grandparents, of the world they were born into and the one they helped create. And while some of the events described here happened in faraway places decades ago, you will probably recognize that some things are the way they are now because of what happened then. In other words, this is not only your parents' and grandparents' story; it is your story, too.

One of the most important reasons to study history is to help us understand the present. Think of how old you are today. Now think about your parent or grandparent or even great-grandparent at your age. Without so much as blinking, you can list five things that did not exist in their lifetime. At the beginning of the twentieth century, there was no automobile, no television, no radio, and certainly no Internet. African Americans in the South lived in segregated communities; few women worked outside the home, and none had the right to vote. So how did we get here from there?

Consider global affairs. When your parents and grandparents were growing up, America's biggest enemy was the Soviet Union, which included modern-day Russia and neighboring countries. From the end of World War II in 1945 until 1991, when the Soviet Union collapsed under its own weight, America and the Soviet Union often stood nose to nose. In what we now refer to as the Cold War, a nuclear confrontation between the two countries was a persistent threat, though thankfully, one that was never realized.

Today, the Soviet Union is long gone, replaced, in one sense, by America's twenty-first-century enemy: radical factions of the religion of Islam. Yet you will be interested to read about the events of 1979, when rebels inspired by the Ayatollah Ruhollah Khomeini, the long-exiled spiritual leader of Iranian Shiite

Muslims, challenged what he called the decadent West by overthrowing the American-backed Shah of Iran and installing an anti-American regime. Looking back, we can now say that when Khomeini's followers seized the American embassy in Tehran and held 52 people hostage for 444 days, they gave us a hint of what was to come twenty-some years later: the events of September 11, 2001, the wars in Iraq and Afghanistan, and the threat of Islamic terrorism that you live with today. If you were a small child on September 11, 2001 (or not yet born), that date may seem like just another landmark in our history. But for many others, it is the defining moment of the twenty-first century, *their* twenty-first century. These books will help you understand this and other world-shattering events that shaped our lives.

Another way to think of history is to say that it is the study of change. Consider this: the adolescents of the early 1900s were not referred to as teenagers—the word wasn't even used until 1941—and as late as 1920, children were unlikely to finish, and often even to start, high school. Teens were needed to work the farms in what was still largely an agricultural society. Certainly no one would have imagined that there could be such a thing as a distinct teen culture. The rise of popular music, which came with the phonograph and then the radio, made such a culture possible. So did urbanization, industrialization, and prosperity, which by the 1950s gave families the luxury to let young people stay in school longer, maybe even go to college, and to be "teenagers."

Technology has always been among the biggest agents of change, and as the story of the twentieth century shows, it can introduce itself unexpectedly. When Henry Ford built the first affordable cars in the United States, he imagined that he was creating a machine that would enhance rural life. The first Model Ts had the potential to double as farm tractors. But in the end the automobile had the opposite effect: once people could get into their Fords and travel, they could see worlds that had long been beyond them, and so a kind of new mobility entered American life, with children growing up and moving far away to pursue lives wholly different from those of their parents. Similarly, the first computers— room-sized behemoths created in the late 1940s— were designed almost exclusively as tools for the scientific community, not as the research, communication, and entertainment platforms we consider them today. It was not until the early 1980s that most people had computers in their offices and homes.

The technological, intellectual, and commercial explosions that greeted the twentieth century made many people dream of a day when a permanent harmony would descend over the globe, but sadly, that was not to be. In fact, if there was one common teenage experience the world over, it was that most ancient of human activities, war. Beginning in 1914, large armies in Europe engaged in horrific battle. People called that first global conflict the Great War, thinking that it would be the last such battle in human history. Now we call it World War I, followed as it was by World War II, just twenty years later, and by the persistent late-twentieth-century (and now early-twenty-first-century) fears that we were (or are) on the brink of World War III.

More than nine million people, much of Europe's youth, died in the Great War alone. But as you contemplate such numbing numbers, it may be more powerful to think not just about how many lives were lost, but also about whose lives were lost. If there had been no war in 1914, maybe one of those who died would have grown up to be a scientist who discovered a cure for cancer or a humanitarian who solved the world's hunger problem. Maybe Germans, absent the humiliation of defeat, would never have listened to the perverse racist message of Adolf Hitler, who led that country into the nightmare that could be stopped only by an even greater war that killed even more people. Many historians are now convinced that had there been no World War I, there would likely have been no World War II and no Cold War, for each, it seems, led inevitably to the next.

With all its wars and devastation, the twentieth century may seem like a bleak episode, a sad study. But as you continue your journey through these three volumes, hold that thought. Loud and sensational events always mask slower, deeper trends, and in the twentieth century the more gradual and less sensational changes mark a time of glorious achievement.

Because the forces of liberty did win that protracted battle between East and West, there are more people living in free and democratic societies today than at any time in human history. In our own country, freedom was extended to millions who had long been denied it by persistent traditions of racial, gender, and ethnic discrimination. Only after defeating Hitler were the American armed forces, in 1948, desegregated.

Science produced new weapons of frightening magnitude in the twentieth century, but it also found ways to erase disease and prolong life. Perhaps the century's most significant change is represented by this fact: if you had been born in 1905, you could expect to live only forty-nine years. By contrast, babies born in America today, as you read this, will likely live to seventy-eight, and some—many, in fact—will live to see the twenty-second century.

In a century when it sometimes seemed that some life-changing innovation was being introduced every week, there were also many remarkable acts of human will by people who, stuck in situations that seemed utterly hopeless, found the courage to ask "why?" The twentieth century produced so many more heroes than villains, people like Thomas Edison and Bill Gates, Jackie Robinson and Rosa Parks, George Marshall and Martin Luther King Jr., and it no doubt produced many more who never became famous, who moved quietly, even silently, behind the drama to make life better. They pushed for justice and beauty and good and not only asked "why?" but, thinking of how things could be made better, also asked "why not?" I hope all of you reading this book will emerge inspired by their example. As my colleague Peter Jennings used to write when signing the original edition of *The Century for Young People,* "The next century is yours." To that, I would add a challenge: "Make your mark on it."

—Todd Brewster

CHAPTER 1

Over the Edge

1936–1941

A nail-biting sense of dread dominated life in the late 1930s. Everywhere people looked, there was proof that things were going very wrong. The American economy was still limping along, with little to show for FDR's New Deal programs. Yet even as people in the United States struggled to put food on the table and keep a roof over their heads, there were rumblings of war from around the globe. In 1936 Italy's dictator, Benito Mussolini, seized Ethiopia. In Spain another dictator, Francisco Franco, began a brutal civil war that would eventually bring him to power. In 1937 the Japanese began attacks on China. And Germany's Adolf Hitler was threatening to take over neighboring Czechoslovakia.

These world events felt closer to home than ever before because of the way news was delivered. Instead of reading about incidents in newspapers days after they happened, Americans turned on their radios for daily news flashes. Live broadcasts from Spain brought the sounds of exploding bombs into American living rooms. Whole families sat by their radios listening to the frightening sounds coming from Europe.

Bob Trout, who was born in 1908, was one of the early news broadcasters who brought world events home to America.

In the middle of the 1930s neither of the two big radio networks—NBC and CBS—had a news department. All we did was air a couple of five-minute news broadcasts a day, which were supplied by the Press Radio Bureau. But toward the end of the decade the country began to count on getting its news from us.

It was a standard evening ritual in houses: People would gather round these rather large radio sets when the news came on, and nobody would talk very much until it was over. They listened to H. V. Kaltenborn bringing them coverage of the Spanish Civil War with the crackle of the rifles in the distance, and certainly nobody had ever heard real gunfire on the air before. Radio was bringing things right into people's homes, and it was beginning to affect the way people felt about what was going on in the world. So when something important happened in Europe, the country was prepared to listen. Americans had always been somewhat interested in Europe's affairs, but they just didn't feel that they were intimately affected by them. Now they were fascinated.

When Hitler annexed Austria, we did a full half hour of reports from Europe, with correspondents in Paris, Berlin, Washington, and London, and me in New York, acting as what would now be called an anchorman. Then in 1939 came the Czech crisis, which was a major radio event, and the country was enthralled by it all. They listened as much as they possibly could. It's no exaggeration to say that radio brought the whole country together, all at the same instant, everyone listening to the same things. And the country liked being tied together that way. In the morning people would say, "Did you hear that last night? Did you hear Hitler speaking again? What was he talking about? Did you hear them all cheering, 'Sieg heil'? What did you think?" It was on the tip of everybody's tongue. People didn't quite see just yet exactly how all these things overseas were ever going to intimately affect their daily lives. But it was the greatest show they'd ever been offered.

Still, few Americans were interested in seeing their country get involved in another war in Europe. Times were tough enough at home. The country's attention was focused inward, not outward. Just as new technology such as radio brought Americans closer to events in Europe, it also brought them closer to each other. A new sense of "we" encouraged Americans to celebrate their own country. And a new sense of "we" also energized workers. The 1930s were a period of resentment between the working class and the industrialists. Because of the Depression, jobs were hard to find, and working men and women were afraid to make demands. But in 1935 Congress passed the National Labor Relations Act, a law that gave unions bargaining power and encouraged workers to organize and demand better wages and working conditions.

Victor Reuther, born in 1912, was one of the first union organizers to fight for the rights of working men and women.

For me, the most exciting aspect of the mid-1930s was the growth of industrial unionism and the birth of the CIO [Congress of Industrial Organizations]. By "industrial unionism" I mean a concept of unionism that embraced the skilled, the semiskilled, and the unskilled as members of the same union. This was in great contrast to the old tradition of the AF of L [American Federation of Labor], which sought to unionize only the skilled elite. The way the AF of L saw it, unskilled factory workers didn't earn enough to pay dues, so why bother? By contrast, industrial unionists were committed to the well-being of the lowest paid, and also to the idea of bridging the racial gap. Black people worked beside whites in the coal fields, the steel mills, and auto and rubber factories.

The rise of the CIO was one of the most dramatic chapters in the history of labor—not only in the United States but in the world. But what came as the real surprise was how quickly the workers in mining, steel, rubber, and auto responded to the idea of organizing. I know this came as a surprise to me and my brother, Walter Reuther, at the level we were organizing in Detroit.

I think I can best describe this rapid growth by telling the story of the factory in which I was working in the fall of 1936. There were five thousand workers in these two plants on the west side of Detroit. And we had all of seventy-eight members signed up in the union. I was working in a department that had a higher percentage of union membership than any others—though still not great. And there was a Polish woman working at the punch press next to me who had two small children at home, and I knew she worried about them. But the speed of the line and the pressure on all of the workers in there was so horrible in those days that it caused her to faint one day. And visibly, she dramatized a problem that was common to every worker among the five thousand: the incredible pressure under which they were working. There was a look of awe and bewilderment on the face of every worker in that department as they looked at this woman. And they were angry. And I came home and I reported to my brother what had happened that day. And he said, I want to meet with this woman.

We went to see her at home, and Walter said to her, "It is time we do something dramatic to overcome the workers' fear of organizing. Do you think you can faint again, but this time on schedule?" She looked at him with bewilderment. "Not Monday, but Tuesday. Give us a day to work on this." She promised to do it. Tuesday came, and sure enough she went into a dead faint. I walked over and pulled the main switch, and gradually all these huge presses ground to a frightening silence. It was an awesome silence, because the workers had never been in the factory when it was quiet before. And suddenly, they realized the incredible power they had in their own hands. They could shut the place down, and they did. And the strike began.

We had a ten-day strike. But as a result of that first stoppage that grew out of the woman fainting, we could not sign up workers fast enough. Fear was eliminated, wiped out in one dramatic move. Soon we had over three thousand workers signed up. Ours was a short and quick strike, but we won, and we raised our wages in one simple move from twenty-two and thirty-three cents an hour to a minimum of seventy-five cents an hour for everyone—blacks, women, it didn't matter. We were on our way.

Even as Americans focused on improving their own lives, it was getting harder for them to ignore the bloody deeds of the dictators across the Atlantic. On April 26, 1937, a squadron of German planes flew over the tiny Spanish town of Guernica. It was market day, and the town was filled with people from surrounding villages. The German planes were there to support Franco in the civil war, and that afternoon they ruthlessly bombed the town for three hours. Women carrying babies, shop owners, peasants—more than sixteen hundred people were killed. Guernica was not an important military target; the reason for the bombing was to terrorize the Spanish people. It succeeded in terrifying people around the world. Was this how battles would now be fought, with bombs raining down on children?

It was becoming more and more obvious that Hitler's policies were aimed at threatening people as much as governments or armies. In the spring of 1938 the Germans marched into Austria in an invasion that met almost no challenge from the Austrian people. Hitler called it the Anschluss, or "union." Within days, Austria was completely transformed into an extension of the Nazi Reich. Shops owned by Jews were looted, and synagogues were occupied by soldiers. As crowds taunted them with insults, Jews were made to scrawl anti-Semitic slogans across their own storefronts, or to get down on their knees to scrub anti-Nazi graffiti from the sidewalks. Policemen even forced them to clean toilets using their precious prayer bands, or tefillin, in place of rags.

Karla Stept, who was born in 1918, saw her world end when the Nazis marched into Vienna.

The winter before the Anschluss was a great time. We were happy, we danced the nights away, we made plans for the future.

It never occurred to us that, as Jews, something bad could happen to us. Austria had always been an anti-Semitic country, but in a way it had never really touched us in Vienna. We thought that this was the place where we were born, that this was our country. Every time we heard about what was going on with Hitler in Germany, we said, "Oh, that can't stay that way. They'll get rid of that lunatic." And we believed it. That was our tragedy.

A few weeks before the Anschluss, the chancellor of Austria had gone to see Hitler, and when he came back, he spoke on the radio and told us that there would be no changes, that Austria would always be Austria. We believed it, and we were lulled into thinking that everything was going to be just fine. So when we heard on the radio that German troops had crossed the border into Austria and were met by throngs of people welcoming them with flowers, we were very much surprised. There were Nazi signs everywhere. There were large groups of men in brown uniforms and the SS in their black uniforms, wearing their Nazi armbands. They unfurled enormous swastika banners on all of the official buildings.

We found out later that everything was prepared down to the very last detail. Many

Austrians, it seems, had wanted to be part of Germany, especially those who had Nazi inclinations. They knew exactly what would happen, but they thought they would be much better off. The Germans came to Austria and trained people who wanted to be Nazis, though the Nazi Party was illegal at that time. All the preparation had to go on without anybody knowing, and I'm sure today that they trained tens of thousands of people.

So Austria converted to Nazism within an hour. It was unbelievable. Then the telephones began to hum. People who lived in sections of the city where they could see what was going on would call and say, "Don't go out. Stay in. You don't know what will happen to you." We were all on the phones to each other. "Is everything all right? What are you doing? What's going on? Look out the window. What's going on on the streets?" Because we weren't sure what was going on.

On Saturday morning, twenty-four hours after the German troops had crossed the border, the brown shirts and the black shirts got to work against the Jewish population of Vienna. They forced Jewish men and women to get down on their knees and scrub the sidewalks free of graffiti, all the while being kicked by the people standing around them. They put detergents and other things into the water, which would eat away at the skin, so these people had to scrub with bleeding hands. And seeing the faces of the bystanders, it was terrible. They were enjoying it. They really enjoyed what was happening to those poor people.

In November 1938 the violence spread. Distraught over the suffering of his family at the hands of the Nazis, a young Jew named Herschel Grynszpan walked into the German embassy in Paris and shot a diplomat, Ernst vom Rath. When word of the murder reached Germany, it enraged the Nazi leadership. The minister of propaganda ordered troops into the streets for a night of violent attacks against the Jews. In Berlin, Stuttgart, Vienna, and other cities, crowds smashed the windows of stores owned by Jews and broke into Jewish homes, looting, burning, and attacking. One hundred and eleven Jews were killed and 177 synagogues were destroyed in what came to be known as Kristallnacht, the "Night of Broken Glass."

In Hamburg, Ralph Giordano, born in 1923, witnessed the terror of Kristallnacht.

Kristallnacht is a term that minimizes the event. It would be better to call it the "night of the imperial pogrom." That night was a clear turning point, a great divide, the beginning of a new era, and not only for the Jews. My family was not bothered on that night. But the next morning, on the way to school, there was a very strange, totally altered atmosphere. One could tell that the people were stirred up, that something had happened that was entirely new. And then I found out at school what had happened. There were some Nazis in my class, and they were happy, rubbing their hands together, saying, "Now the Jews will be dealt with, finally the time has come." And then after school, I went into the center of Hamburg, and I saw what damage had been done. It was so monstrous that you didn't want to believe it. It was like a terrible dream. Windows were shattered, goods were scattered in the street. There was smoke and fire. Merchandise was thrown out onto the street. There were people who walked in the midst of it without any self-consciousness at all, who showed themselves to be completely indifferent. There were also other people who you could tell were troubled. They kept their heads down and were probably extremely disturbed by what they saw. And from that point in time, everything was clear. It was plain that the Nazi regime was capable of doing anything. Suddenly there was the feeling that we could meet with a violent death at any moment, not because we did anything against the system, against the regime, but because we existed in the world as Jews, because of our biological existence. This feeling was very tangible, very palpable from that moment on.

After Kristallnacht, there was outrage in the United States. Americans called for harsh sanctions against Germany. In Congress there was an effort to widen immigration quotas to let in more German Jews fleeing the Nazis. Robert Wagner, a senator from New York, introduced a bill that would have admitted ten thousand German Jewish children. But the bill failed, and in the end, the country did very little to support the Jews. Many people saw the acceptance of more European immigrants as a mistake. America was still suffering from the Great Depression, and refugees from Europe might take precious jobs away from Americans.

Many Americans tried their best to ignore what was happening overseas. They looked for an escape from their worries through entertainment. One of the biggest and flashiest distractions was the World's Fair, held in New York City in 1939–40. The pavilions of thirty-three states, fifty-eight foreign countries (minus Nazi Germany), and thirteen hundred businesses dazzled visitors with such marvels as television, nylon stockings, robots, and man-made lightning. "I have seen the future" was one motto at the fair, and people flocked to New York to get a peek.

Gilda Snow, born in 1929, visited the fair at the end of the summer of 1939.

M y father was an electrician, and when I was about eight or nine he wanted to show me the kind of stuff he did. So he brought me to the place where he was working, and it turned out to be the New York World's Fair! My father took me around to all the buildings and exhibits that were starting to go up, and he said, "This is what I do, kid. This is it! And someday this place is all going to be lit up."

When the fair opened officially, it was quite an event, with lots of people there, of course. The crowds really gathered there because I think American people were ready for a pick-me-up. Everyone had been down in the dumps for so long from the Depression, and this World's Fair was helping everybody come alive again. Being at the fair was like having a bird's-eye view of the future, and people loved it.

There were all kinds of exhibits—Wonder bread, where they gave you a little loaf of bread; Heinz, where they gave you a little green pickle pin to wear. But the fair was called the "World of Tomorrow," and the most interesting exhibits were the ones that showed you what the future would be like. I remember sitting in a dark room and watching a rotating stage that would display first the old and then the new. We would see all the old washing machines, refrigerators, cars, and so on, and then little by little the stage would move, and we would be in the future. There were televisions, electric washers, electric dryers—everything was electrified. It was almost like a fairy tale, like a whole different way of living. It was so easy. Take the refrigerator, for example. It made its own ice. You didn't have to do anything with it except open and close it! And there was a light inside of it! There was a television demonstration where this man would film you. And to see your picture on the screen, well, that was just unbelievable. How it worked, we did not know. I didn't even ask! I was just in awe of the whole thing. It was hard to believe that we would ever see any of these things, because, let's face it, at that time we were just pulling ourselves out of a depression.

But then I remember going to the Polish pavilion. We were going up this huge, beautiful walkway, with flowers all around us. But as soon as we got up to the building, the lights went out. My father, he figured they had an electrical short, because the rest of the fair was all lit up. And then we heard over a loudspeaker that Germany had just invaded Poland and that they were closing down that pavilion. And that, of course, was the beginning of the war. I remember thinking, "War? Where?" I didn't even know where Poland was at that time. But there wasn't anything to see and we couldn't go into the pavilion, so we just walked away from it.

In late August, startling news came over the radio. Hitler and Stalin had signed an agreement that split Poland into two spheres of influence, with Germany poised on its western side and the Soviet Union looming over it from the east. Then at dawn on September 1, 1939, Hitler faked a Polish invasion of Germany to give himself an excuse for fighting back. A million and a half German soldiers were waiting on the German-Polish border for the order to attack.

When the signal came, German tanks rolled across the Polish countryside. The Polish army, still fighting on horseback, was almost powerless to resist. The frontier fell in a few days. Thousands of German soldiers, who had left Berlin in railroad cars painted with the slogan We're Off to Poland to Thrash the Jews!, now descended in tanks and troop carriers on Poland's capital, Warsaw. Wave upon wave of Stuka dive-bombers blasted road junctions and railroad lines. The Stukas, which emitted a piercing shriek that spread terror wherever they went, were backed up by heavy bombers, which pounded the city to rubble. Together, the tanks and bombers carried out the German blitzkrieg, or "lightning war." They hit both military and civilian targets. Within weeks, the Russians invaded Poland from the east to take their share of the spoils. Poland was finished.

Peter Pechel, born in 1920, was part of the invading German army.

Just before the invasion of Poland, Hitler sent the 3rd Armored Division through Berlin, and he was very disappointed by people's reactions. He thought they would be jubilant, as apparently the Germans had been in 1914 when World War I started. But the

Berliners lined the streets and let the tanks go by, remaining totally silent. There was no movement, no reaction, nothing. I think this illustrates the general feeling among the people at that time, especially the young men in uniform, like myself, who would have to use their weapons sooner or later.

Not long after that, my company marched into Czechoslovakia and camped out on the Polish border. We were very scared because we didn't know what war was. We had only been told by our fathers that war was a horrible thing. And so we hoped and prayed that we would be spared. Then the order came to move into battle position. We were to march across the border at 4:45 A.M. on the first of September, 1939. For a young man, war means hearing the first shots, and suddenly having strange smells in your nose: burning houses, burning cows, burning dogs, burning corpses. It means seeing the first people killed; in Poland it was civilians. And then seeing young men like yourself in foreign uniforms being killed or wounded.

I was in an armored tank division, and of course we rode on and on and just kept on rolling. We were the spearhead of the German army. The Poles were very tough to fight. They fought bitterly and desperately.

But it was easy for a modern army like the German army to beat them, because here we were in tanks being attacked by the Polish cavalry. Can you imagine? Soldiers on horses with lances moved against tanks.

Julian Kulski, born in 1929, described the effects of the blitzkrieg on the Polish countryside.

In the summer of 1939 my father, who was the mayor of Warsaw, rented a house out in the Polish countryside because he knew the war was coming soon. One day I was playing in the woods with my friend, and we heard this tremendous sound of motors, and watched the trees start bending. Huge planes with sinister-looking black crosses on them were flying over us, pretty much at the level of the treetops. They were headed north, toward Warsaw, and they must have been one of the first squadrons of the Luftwaffe. This was when I realized that war had begun, and it was a terrifying experience.

The little medieval town near us was bombed a few days later. And since it was not defended, the Wehrmacht took it over immediately. I was near the market when I first saw them coming, and while I expected something like cavalry on horses, they came on motorcycles and trucks. They wore greatcoats covered with dust, goggles, and very scary gray helmets. Somehow I expected that the invader would come in looking very well dressed, but they looked pretty beaten up and bedraggled. The Polish army had given them a hard resistance on the border, so they had been fighting every day. They put up a field gun in the middle of the square near the cathedral. They brought in a large military band and started playing "*Deutschland über Alles*" and other German marching songs.

At the same time, they started a fire in the synagogue and tied up the rabbi, letting the elders run into the temple to try to save him. My first impression was this was complete unreality. And absolute horror.

I didn't stay in that town very long, but before we left, I remember that a nine-year-old peasant boy came over and touched the handle of a German motorcycle. And a soldier, who was inside the café, came out and shot him dead, right in front of my eyes. After that I stayed away from Germans, period.

In spite of the terror being unleashed in Europe, American isolationists, those who wanted the United States to keep to itself, were still a loud voice. Nevertheless, Americans followed the progress of the war with great interest. While Hitler took

Denmark and then Norway, maps sold out across the United States. People mounted them on their walls and, listening to the news flashes on their radios, marked the troop movements. But that didn't mean they wanted America to get involved.

Bob Stuart, born in 1916, was a student at Yale University who believed that Europe's troubles were not our concern.

Growing up in the thirties, I was educated by people who were seriously disillusioned about why we'd fought in World War I. So the general feeling of my generation was that we shouldn't do that again, especially during a time when we were just pulling ourselves out of a terribly tough depression. When I was in college in 1937 I traveled all through Europe and saw everything that was going on there, and I came back from that trip sort of wondering if all of their problems were really our problems. I was young, and hardly thinking profoundly about anything, but my overall reaction to it all was just, "God, it's great to be an American."

The following year the war clouds were gathering in Europe. As I talked about it among my friends, we began to think about what we could do to keep America from getting trapped in another European war. They were in a mess over there—France seemed disorganized, and the British didn't seem to have too much military capability either, but we felt that fundamentally it was not our concern as Americans. We were just convinced, after the experience of "trying to make the world safe for democracy" in World War I, that we'd better take care of our hemisphere first and avoid entanglements.

In retrospect, it's clear that some of the events going on in Europe, such as Kristallnacht, really didn't get the coverage they deserved. So our awareness level wasn't very high. Dorothy Thompson would write a column from time to time on the refugee situation, but I don't think we were aware of how serious that was. I think we all would have been horrified if we'd really known and understood it.

In the spring of 1940 my friends and I started to worry about President Roosevelt, because it was clear to all of us that he was anxious to help Britain and France. Everything he was doing seemed to lead toward more support and more involvement. We felt very strongly that there was still a lot to rebuild and do in the United States.

President Roosevelt was troubled that America's old allies, Britain and France, faced the growing threat from Germany alone. Yet American support for involvement in Europe wasn't strong enough to let him act. By the spring of 1940 Hitler was moving westward, toward France. His army plowed through Holland, unleashing a wave of civilian terror that forced thousands upon thousands to flee ahead of the tanks and troops. Belgium was next, and the Allied soldiers rose in force to meet the Germans there. Unfortunately, they fell into a deadly trap.

Most of the French army was in the trenches of the Maginot Line, which had been built in the 1930s to defend France from the west. (They had expected, mistakenly, that the next war would be fought much like the last one.) With most of the British army in Belgium, Hitler sent his troops into France from the north, in between the two Allied armies. The Allied forces in Belgium found themselves nearly surrounded, and the only strategy left to them was to retreat. Britain's prime minister, Winston Churchill, ordered his troops to flee to Dunkirk, the French port that was now their only way out. He sent 165 ships of the Royal Navy to meet them there, but the waters were too shallow for the navy vessels. London put out an emergency call for any boat that could cross the English Channel and rescue the soldiers. Some 850 yachts, fishing boats, ferries, and firefighting boats responded, while the Luftwaffe descended on the town, pounding the beaches with machine-gun fire and bombs.

Paule Rogalin, born in 1930, was a little girl in Dunkirk who saw the Luftwaffe's attack.

Just before the war began I was living in Dunkirk with my mother. My father had been drafted and was stationed nearby. Since so many of the French ships were coming through Dunkirk we saw soldiers all of the time, and we just knew something bad was going to happen soon. It was like living on dynamite. All of us children went to school each day with a gas mask on our back, a school bag, and a blanket, because there was no heat in the classrooms due to shortages.

One night my mother and I went to see some friends in the port of Dunkirk. We started to hear these loud explosions, but the air raid signal had not sounded, so we didn't know what it was. And suddenly we were surrounded by fire. The big ships in the harbor were on fire, and men were jumping off them—some of the men were on fire as well. We were so shocked, we ran and jumped into a ditch shelter nearby. The bombs kept falling, and soon the shelter started collapsing. I was almost up to my nose in dirt. I was getting buried alive. And these three young men got my hands, and they pulled me out of the dirt.

We ran toward the town of Dunkirk, but bombs were just falling all over. It was terrible. It's something I cannot forget. Houses were collapsing, and we could hear people down in the basement who were screaming because they were drowning in the water from pipes that had burst. And we just kept on running. It seemed like we ran almost all night.

In the morning the bombing stopped for a while, so we started walking back to our house. It was still standing up, but as we got nearer, we could see the drapes flying out of the windows, and we could see that a bomb had exploded inside the house. We stayed there for a few days, because there was nowhere else to go; the whole city of Dunkirk was just gone, all gone. We kept hearing that the German soldiers were marching toward our town.

Though I can't remember the first German I saw, I do remember the sound of their boots and their voices. That's what scared me the most. They came into our house, which was half gone, and they kept saying to my mother, "Where is the man of the house?" They thought we were hiding something. And she kept telling them he was in the French army. I guess they wanted to take him prisoner. I'm not a hateful person, but I felt hatred toward the Germans. I hated them with a passion. And I felt like we were not French anymore. We were invaded by these people, who had done so much damage and so much killing, and I'm sure a lot of them got killed, too, but at that point I didn't care.

After a few days we left the house, bringing with us a few things that we carried on our backs. When we got onto the main road we saw that many others were doing the same thing. We looked for our friends but we couldn't find them. As we walked along we saw a lot of dead people; I remember seeing one man who had burned up inside his truck, and he was still at the wheel. Then the enemy started shooting at us from their airplanes, and even though we were mostly just women, children, and old people, they would swoop down low and shoot at us. We had to scramble down the hill into the canal in order to avoid getting hit.

We saw French soldiers in trenches who had no idea what to do. They were lost just like we were, running in all directions with no general to tell them what to do. When my father managed to find us, he was just like those men. He had left the army because they had no guns, nothing to fight with. He was almost crying when he found us, saying, "We can't fight. We don't have anything."

Many people in France saw the retreat from Dunkirk as a betrayal. But the makeshift fleet saved 200,000 British soldiers and 140,000 French soldiers. It also gave the Allies time to regroup in England. France fell in a few days, and utter chaos reigned on the European continent. From Paris alone, more than two million people had fled in cars and on bicycles and on foot, pushing baby carriages and wagons. They wandered the countryside, searching for someplace to hide from the Germans.

Now that Hitler was in command of Europe, Italy's Mussolini joined him. Japan was impressed by Hitler, too. Soon Italy, Germany, and Japan signed an agreement forming the Axis alliance. Only penniless Britain was left to stand against them. But Britain, short on money and weapons, had found in Winston Churchill a man who could inspire the nation. His dramatic speeches gave English men and women new hope. "Victory," he promised them. "Victory at all costs. Victory in spite of all terror. Victory, however hard and long the road may be, for without victory there is no survival."

In July 1940 the island safety of Britain was destroyed by bombers launched from France. The Luftwaffe, the German air force, was preparing the way for a full-scale invasion. To the Germans' great surprise, the Royal Air Force fought back bravely. Over the cliffs of Dover, British Spitfires engaged in fierce air combat with German Messerschmitts. But then the bombers began striking at the heart of Britain: London itself.

From September to November nearly 250 bombers attacked London each night, sending people running into air raid shelters and subway stations for safety. Entire blocks of houses were demolished. Factories were gutted. Every morning there were mounds of smoking rubble, deep bomb craters, dead bodies, and workers busy cleaning up the debris so that life could go on.

Sheila Black, who was born in 1920, remembers the London blitz.

Most of us learned that the war had begun when we heard it on the radio. There was kind of silence before it and after it, or at least that's how it seems in my memory. It was a very short announcement: "We are now at war with Germany." But, of course, what was a war? Was it going to be the war of World War I, when soldiers got shipped over and walked through trenches and tried to shoot the enemy, or what? We had no idea, and we certainly didn't know then how much of the war would be in the air, right over our heads.

First the men were called to join the military. Then there was the building of the air raid shelters. In our gardens we got Anderson shelters, which were tin huts buried under the earth. And in our homes we got what were called Morrison shelters, which were wrought-iron tables. We were to hide under these tables if there was a bomb. We also had to line all of our curtains with black fabric, to make sure our homes were absolutely light-tight. There was a group of men called the Home Guard who kept watch for bombs or other signs of invasion, and we were rather led to believe that at any moment a German might parachute himself into our midst. So there was a national feeling that we had to be ready.

We were all issued gas masks, which were horrid things with eyepieces, which you looked through, and long snouts, which you breathed through. They were bad enough as it was, but what was worse was the contraption they gave you for your baby. It was an enormous cabinet into which you fastened your child. And you had to pump fresh air into this for the baby to breathe. Ugh! They were horrible things, and I think they made me feel more like we were in a war than almost anything else. The toddlers got what was called a Mickey Mouse gas mask, which was the same as the adult model, but painted like Mickey Mouse.

I was married when the war actually started, and pregnant when the dogfights over Kent and London began. Then came the bombing. On the night of September 14, 1940, London was ablaze and the docks were alight. That was the night I went into labor. Our flat was at the end of a car park where antiaircraft guns were positioned. So the noise was absolutely deafening when the battle started. My midwife rode over on her bicycle at around midnight, and she stayed through the night because it wasn't safe for her to leave. My daughter was born at three o'clock that morning, and the midwife opened the curtains because we got more bright light from London burning than we got from the electric light in the middle of the room. That was the Battle of Britain, and that, for us, was truly the beginning of the war.

What else is there to say about the blitz? Yes, there was bombing, yes, we lived with it, yes, we woke up and some areas were devastated, but we got used to it. You lived for the day. And then at night you would get under your Morrison shelter, into which you put your mattress. And you got into bed with the children. And others packed up their mattresses and blankets and went down into the tube stations. And when you came up in the morning, you saw dead people. You would think we would have all been terribly squeamish about it, but we got used to it. Human beings are extraordinarily resilient. They get used to anything. Or almost anything.

Across the Atlantic, many Americans, with FDR's guidance, were beginning to change their minds about this war. While London burned, isolationists and interventionists debated America's responsibilities to the Allies. And while they argued, Hitler's relentless aggression continued. In the spring of 1941 he broke his agreement with Stalin and marched his troops into the Soviet Union. In less than a month the Germans advanced more than three hundred miles into Soviet territory.

Perhaps it was because most Americans were of European ancestry, or perhaps it was because Hitler riveted the country's attention. But more Americans were focusing their attention on Europe than on Japan in 1941. That all changed on Sunday, December 7.

In the early hours of that day, 189 Japanese bombers lifted off from ships in the Pacific Ocean. They were headed for the American naval base at Pearl Harbor in Hawaii. When they neared their target, the squadron leader spotted Battleship Row. He signaled for the bombers to begin their surprise attack. Within minutes Pearl Harbor was an inferno, as battleships, destroyers, supply ships, and cruisers went up in flames. When the assault was finished, the United States was left with 2,433 dead, 1,178 wounded, 18 warships sunk, and 188 planes destroyed. It was the worst day in American naval history.

Now there was no doubt as to America's point of view. Armed with grim resolve, the country would go to war, in Europe and in Asia. Army recruiting stations were jammed within hours of the catastrophe in Hawaii. As President Roosevelt said, December 7 was a date that would "live in infamy." The United States treated the attack as an invasion: It was a blow that must be swiftly returned.

CHAPTER 2

Global Nightmare

1941–1945

From 1941 to 1945 the world experienced the most terrible period of modern times. The war that had raged in Europe for more than two years now spiraled out of control, becoming a truly global conflict. Americans were fighting against the Japanese in the Pacific and joining the Allies to face off against the Germans in the Atlantic, in North Africa, and in Europe itself.

The stakes had been raised. No longer did it seem that the war was being fought only to stop the advance of Germany. Now it was a fight to prevent the destruction of the world·as people knew it, and the combat had no limits. Civilians had become targets, and millions of innocent people perished.

Amazingly, millions also fought back. Struggling to survive, they enjoyed the one satisfaction that was left for them: the sense of companionship and purpose that came with fighting a war against evil—and fighting it together.

The entire populations of the warring countries were involved. Women worked in munitions factories, men flew lonely combat missions, and children collected materials for scrap drives. Yet the sense that this was "total war" developed not just because whole societies were involved. "Total war" captured the feeling of global madness that the war produced. Even after it was over and the Allies had triumphed, people wondered if the evil forces that Hitler represented had somehow won, too—because now there was a sense that the world had gone somewhere it could never return from. People had seen things they would never be able to forget.

After Pearl Harbor, there was no question left for Americans: The country must join the war. By February 1942 more than five million volunteers had joined community war efforts. Industry moved into high gear, churning out so many tanks, planes, guns, and ships that the economy was pushed out of the Depression.

The attack on Pearl Harbor was a unique moment in modern American history. An enemy had slipped across our borders, and it affected people the way a burglary at home does: They never felt totally safe again. Everyone was afraid. Weather reports were stopped for fear that enemy fliers might use them to plan attacks. Man-on-the-street interviews were ended for fear that someone might blurt out a national secret. Thousands of Japanese Americans were forced to leave their homes and move into detention camps, for fear that they might try to help the enemy.

In the months after the Japanese attack on Pearl Harbor, the American forces in the Pacific were defeated again and again. Wake Island, Guam, Borneo, Singapore, and the Philippines all fell. Nearly half of the Pacific air force was destroyed. Even though these islands were far away, Americans at home were convinced that their own lives were in danger. And although they were afraid, they also wanted revenge.

This time, though, there were no cheerful tunes urging men to go into battle. The experiences of World War I had taught these soldiers and their families what war really meant. People were ready to fight, but they knew it would be an ugly job.

President Roosevelt defined America's war goals in terms everyone could understand. He called them the Four Freedoms: freedom from want, freedom from fear, freedom of belief, and freedom of expression. These were goals people were willing to work hard to achieve.

By the time American factories were running at peak production, cargo ships that used to take a year to build were being constructed in seventeen days. Bombers came off the line fifteen times faster than usual. A typewriter factory switched over to producing machine guns, and a corset company made grenade belts. With so many men at war, the workforce was flooded with women who took off their aprons and put on overalls. Everyone was pulling part of the load.

Neil Shine, born in 1930, was a boy when America entered the war. His family, like millions of others, pitched in.

In 1941 I was living in Detroit with my parents and my two younger brothers. I came home one Sunday afternoon from the Plaza Theater to a household that was somber and quiet. The radio was on, and I was told that the Japanese had bombed Pearl Harbor. I spent the whole next day talking with other kids about this war and what it would mean, and the excitement level was high. I mean, I was eleven years old, and I just didn't understand that people died in wars and that war was a horrible thing. To us it was simply excitement.

My parents understood what war was. My father was a veteran of the First World War. My brothers and I were constantly asking him questions, but he didn't talk about it much. Once I asked my father, "Did we kill more Germans or did they kill more Americans?" And he didn't answer me for quite a while, but then he said something like, "It's hard to say because dead soldiers are all on the same side." I didn't know what he meant at the time.

To us kids, combat was a sort of lifestyle, with the good guys and the bad guys. And suddenly here was this exciting thing happening, with the good guys versus the bad guys, and we were the good guys and we were going to win! We played war constantly. We constantly roamed the empty fields near our house, attacking the abandoned buildings and hurling clumps of mortar at them. But nobody would be the Japanese, and nobody would be the Germans. We were all the good guys.

We watched the newsreels, the Hollywood version of World War II, with scenes from the battlefields, where we were always winning. We would come out of the movies so fired up. In fact, we even got fired up in the movies. Once during a movie called *Bataan,* we were losing badly to the Japanese, and Lefty Brosnan, one of the kids in the neighborhood, stood up and threw a golf ball at the screen to try to stem the Japanese onslaught. All he did was mess up the screen so that for the rest of the war it had a big patch in it that you could always see there. Eventually the newsreels became so popular that Detroit opened a newsreel theater downtown. It was all flamethrowers and bombs and shells, and we indulged ourselves in this chaos.

We were always on the lookout for spies, so to us, people with foreign accents were automatically suspect. Now, in an immigrant neighborhood, this is pretty ridiculous, right? I mean, my own father had a foreign accent. But we'd pick out people we thought were likely spies because they wore long overcoats and slouch hats.

We all felt Detroit was at risk, as much as anyplace else, that is. The word ENEMY was everywhere, in capital letters. We had to protect our shores from this "enemy." We learned the silhouettes of all the airplanes, and we spent countless hours lying on our backs at the playground, looking skyward, watching for Messerschmitts and Stukas and Mitsubishis and Zeros. But all we ever saw were the planes from the local air base. If they had ever tried to slip one airplane over Detroit airspace, without a doubt some kid in my neighborhood would have sounded the alarm.

My father was an air raid warden, but he

could have been Eisenhower's aide-de-camp and I wouldn't have been any prouder. He had a white helmet with a symbol on it, an armband, a flashlight, and a whistle. We were so absolutely proud of him as we watched him striding up and down the street making people close those drapes and shut off those lights during the air raid drills. We also had air raid drills at school, where we would get under these tables in the basement.

There was this thing called "the war effort" that took on a life of its own; you had to be doing something for it. One day my mother got herself a pair of slacks, a cap that held her hair in the back, and a lunch bucket and went to work in a factory. My mother was this nice lady who baked and cooked and cleaned house and kept her kids in line, and suddenly she was running a machine at an aircraft supply factory. Every day for three years she marched off to Continental Motors and ran a machine, and I think she enjoyed it.

I remember being jealous that I didn't have an older brother. Other kids came to school with patches on their jackets that their brothers had sent them, souvenirs from overseas. I felt deprived because I didn't have an older brother who would send me a German helmet. But then there was a sort of ritual at my Catholic school when someone was killed, where someone would come into the classroom and get the siblings of whoever was the casualty, and then announce the name over the public-address system, you know, that "Jack Callahan had been killed in action," and we would all get up, put our coats on, go next door to church and pray, and then go home. I found myself being thankful that I didn't have a brother who was at risk, so that I wouldn't have to sit with my mother while she wept in church, while they played taps and folded the flag and gave it to her. So the realization that this was not so fun anymore finally came to me when the kids from the neighborhood started dying.

Many of the young men who went into combat never returned. Perhaps the greatest difference in this war—as far as the soldier was concerned—was that it depended on machines more than any war before it. Far more than World War I, World War II made use of the tank and the airplane, and of modern rifles that were capable of firing rapidly at the enemy. But if these new guns could fire faster, they were also less accurate. More powerful weapons, and more of them, meant even greater destruction. The two world wars involved about the same number of fighting men and lasted about the same length of time. Yet more than twice as many people died in World War II.

The Pacific war was especially brutal. To the Japanese soldier, there was no higher duty than fighting for his emperor. Death was thought of as a sublime event, and surrender was an intolerable dishonor. It was considered unmanly, and a soldier who surrendered was less than human. The other side of this philosophy was that a surrendering enemy was also less than human: Captives were to be scorned and abused.

Like the Germans, the Japanese were in the grip of an ideology that regarded all other peoples as inferior. The combination of this racism and their contempt for captives resulted in behavior that shocked Americans. Its terrible effect was to encourage the opinion that the Japanese themselves were barbaric, less than human, and deserved barbaric treatment. In the end gruesome acts were committed by both sides.

At least some of this behavior was caused by the strange conditions of the war in the Pacific. Most of these battles happened far from signs of civilization, on tiny coral-reef islands that seemed almost like another planet.

Earle Curtis, born in 1918, was a private in the Marine Corps. He suffered from shell shock during a battle in the Pacific, though he later received a citation for bravery.

I was sent with my regiment to Tarawa in the Gilbert Islands. A battle was going on there on one square mile of sand. We arrived on the third day of the battle. It was scorching hot, and corpses were piled everywhere. I was the telephone man, which meant I had to string telephone wire from the command post to where the company was.

We advanced about two hundred yards, and at nightfall we were attacked. Shells were exploding all around me. The first time you get shelled, it's a real rush. Especially when a piece of shrapnel bounces off your shoe or something like that. But the power of high explosives is very demoralizing, because it's this sudden force which has nothing to do with humanity; it's the force of an enormously powerful machine, and there's nothing in the world you can do to resist that. After a while you start to feel like someone who's been in an automobile wreck; you get into a state of shock, and you can't really comprehend everything that's happening around you. There really is no way in the world to prepare yourself for the reality of battle.

During my trips from the front to the rear

of the battle, I was stopped every fifty feet or so by soldiers guarding their shell holes with rifles. I soon realized that all of these shell holes were full of marines who were either wounded or too afraid to go out into battle. The war stories never seem to mention all of these guys who are literally paralyzed with fear, unable or unwilling to fight.

One shell landed so close to me that I was thrown to the ground. When I sat up, I had to pick the pieces of coral gravel out of my face. This was really the climax of my battle experience, and it put me over the thin red line into shell shock. I went and told my captain that I needed a break, and I dug out a little area in a bomb crater and fell asleep. When I woke up a few hours later, a huge noise shook me, and I looked up to see an American fighter plane roaring straight toward me. I wasn't surprised or afraid at all—nothing happening around me seemed to have any bearing on my life. When the plane opened fire I felt the muzzle blast of the machine gun on my face, but I wasn't hit. I scrambled out of my crater and saw that the battlefield had gone quiet.

A shouting voice kind of jolted me into reality; it was a corpsman looking for casualties. He had found a body, and he wanted me to help fix the guy up. I looked down at the man's face and I realized I knew him. His eyes were open, rolling from side to side, the sightless eyes of a dying man. Then I noticed that his right leg was entirely missing. The absurdity of the whole situation suddenly hit me, and I broke into an uncontrolled laugh. All the fear and horror melted away, and I felt nothing but relief. Then suddenly I was sober again. I was watching a man die, and the reality of the violence was back with me. All I could think was, "This is insane, this is too much. Nobody will ever get me to do this again." To live through a battle like Tarawa shakes your faith in humanity forever.

While soldiers were fighting all over the world, ordinary citizens in central Europe and Russia fought for their lives every day in the streets of their cities. In Russia, Hitler had ordered a blockade of the city of Leningrad, hoping to starve its three million people. But even as the Germans bombed warehouses and supply routes to cut off food supplies, Leningrad's citizens showed they would not be easily conquered. People made "bread" with sawdust. They boiled weeds to make soup. Starving people died in the streets and at home, but the city held on.

In Stalingrad the fighting was on the ground, house to house, and in the air. In a single night six hundred German planes dropped bombs that ignited fires throughout the city. But the Russians—soldiers and civilians alike—fought back with everything they had. Housewives fired artillery, snipers crouched on rooftops. Grenades flew from above, behind, and below. The brutal fighting continued for months.

As Hitler's forces rampaged through Russia, SS divisions followed them. Their job was to round up Jews for mass execution. The victims were marched to the countryside, where they were forced to dig their own graves, then were shot. When that method of slaughter proved to undermine the morale of even the hardened Nazi soldiers, they began using mobile gas vans.

At last Hitler's maniacal hatred of the Jews led him to employ what was darkly referred to as the "final solution" to the Jewish "problem." With Germany gaining control all over eastern Europe, Jews from cities and towns were stripped of their belongings and sent to "resettlement camps." These were really death camps. After an initial examination, some were judged fit to work. The rest were ordered into "bathhouses" where what looked like shower-heads actually dispensed Zyklon-B, a poison gas used to kill rats. After they had been gassed, their corpses were hauled off to ovens for burning.

The six most active camps were in Poland, out of sight of the German citizens. The camps took the industrialization of killing to a new level. Now there were not only weapons factories but actual killing factories, too. The staff of Auschwitz, the most notorious of the Polish camps, proudly claimed to be able to "process" twelve thousand inmates a day.

Ernest Michel was born in 1923. He was one of the few survivors of the Auschwitz camp.

I was living in a work camp called Paderborn in northern Germany, cleaning the streets and sewers in the town. We were guarded by policemen, but at least we had something to eat and nobody got shot or killed. In February 1943 we were told to get ready because the entire camp was going to be evacuated toward the east. We walked at night, through the streets we had been cleaning, to the train station, where we were put on cattle cars. We spent five days and five nights in these cars with hardly any food or water, never knowing where we were going. There was no room to sleep or sit down. Several people couldn't take it and they died right in the car; we had to just put them in a corner. Then we came to a place, and somebody called out, "Oświęcim!" That's the Polish word for Auschwitz.

There was a peculiar, sweet smell in the air. I couldn't figure out what it was. We heard noises—dogs barking—and all of a sudden it became very light. The doors of the car were opened up and we heard, "Everybody out. Leave your luggage." Everywhere there was screaming and yelling: "My son, my father, where are you?" We saw for the first time that we were in a line of thirty or forty cars, full of old people, young people, children.

We were forced into two columns, women on one side, men on the other side. I held on to two of my friends. The screaming and yelling continued as mothers looked for their children, and mothers tried to hold on to their babies. I would never have believed that anything like this could happen to human beings, but this was just the beginning. An SS man asked us, "How old?" If you were between the ages of sixteen and thirty, the thumb went up, and you went to one side. Over thirty, the thumb went down, and you went to the other side. The screaming, the whips, the dogs—that picture will be with me as long as I live. "How old?" he asked me. I said, "Nineteen." The thumb went up.

They piled us into trucks, and then a guard said something to me that I didn't understand. He said, "You're the lucky ones. The others are already up the chimney." That's when we started to realize what this place was. All the girls were gassed that same day. But they needed labor, so when the thumb went up, I was given a chance to live. I wasn't hungry anymore. I was scared for my life. "The others are already up the chimney." So that was the smell.

In the morning we were shorn of hair. Then every one of us was tattooed. That's when I got my number, 104995. The normal food rations in Auschwitz were such that you had approximately half a year until your body gave out—they had figured it out very scientifically. And after that, up the chimney.

We didn't live, we existed. That's all it was. The camp was surrounded by two sets of electrically charged wire. The moment you touched it you were electrocuted. I saw inmates by the hundreds run into that barbed wire just to get it over with. But I never wanted to. My parents instilled in me a feeling of responsibility, even during very difficult times. So I told myself and the others around me, some of us have got to hang on in order to tell the story of what happened.

To survive under those circumstances took fortitude and a desire to hang on, but it also took plain old dumb luck. Without a lucky break, something extra that helped you survive, you would never make it. And eventually I got my lucky break. Now, I was getting very thin—probably eighty-five pounds or so—and my bones were starting to show. One day I got hit over the head, and I went to the prison hospital to get taken care of. By some fluke, a man came through the hospital and asked if anyone had good handwriting. Now, in 1939 my father had sent me to take calligraphy lessons. At the time I said, "What do I need this for?" And he said, "You never know when it could come in handy." That ended up saving my life. They sat me down with a logbook and told me what to write: "Weak of body." "Heart attack." The Germans kept immaculate records, and of course nobody was ever gassed. Everybody died of weak body or heart attack. So because I could write neatly I became an official recorder.

Jews weren't the only victims. Gypsies, Slavs, Catholics, homosexuals, and the mentally retarded were sent to their deaths, too. But the Jews were by far the largest group of victims—more than six million Jews died in the Holocaust. Still, when news of the camps began reaching the West in 1942 and 1943, many people found the stories too outrageous to believe. It had to be an exaggeration, they thought; even Hitler could not go that far.

———

By January 1943 the tide of the war began to turn against Germany. Hitler had not planned for a long war, and his factories began to run out of oil and gas. There were other problems, too. The Allies had begun bombing German cities. Now it was German refugees who were clogging the roads searching for shelter. As in London in 1940, people hurried into shelters at night, then rebuilt their homes during the day. All the while they waited for the Allies to launch their land invasion, which everyone knew would come soon.

On the night of June 5, 1944, President Roosevelt announced that the fascists had been defeated in Italy. But Roosevelt was preoccupied. For even as he told Americans this wonderful news, 175,000 Allied soldiers were getting ready on the coast of England for a secret invasion of France. Operation Overlord, as it was called, was an enormous challenge. Along with a massive fighting force, it involved moving fifty thousand motorcycles, tanks, and bulldozers across the sixty miles of the English Channel. It would take more than five thousand ships and eleven thousand airplanes. All told, the operation of D-Day was, one historian noted, like moving the Wisconsin cities of Green Bay, Racine, and Kenosha across Lake Michigan—every man, woman, child, car, and truck—and doing it all in one night. On the morning of June 6, no one was sure it was possible.

As he toured the bases, General Dwight D. Eisenhower, the supreme commander of the Allied troops, went to see off British troops boarding a landing craft. Then he said farewell to twenty-three thousand Allied paratroopers, knowing that experts had predicted that as many as 75 percent of them might be killed. He saluted the planes as they took off for France. Then the tough Kansan who would later become president turned away in tears.

For most Americans D-Day was the climax of the war. People cheered the news of the invasion, which they had eagerly awaited. Churches rang their bells, factories sounded their whistles. Then, just as suddenly, everyone huddled in fear for their young soldiers. Roosevelt went on the radio to do the only thing that he or any other American could do: pray.

In the English Channel, thousands of terrified men from twelve Allied nations floated toward the coast of France, toward beaches code-named Sword, Juno, Omaha, Gold, and Utah. Clair Galdonik, who was born in 1919, was there.

Just before they shipped my infantry unit over to Europe, we were given a ten-day furlough to visit our wives and children. I, being single, went back and spent those ten days with my mother and dad. For me it wasn't a joyful occasion. I didn't tell them that I knew we'd be going into combat; I tried to spare them as much as I could.

When we got to England we were stationed in a huge tent city. We got there in March of 1944 and trained a bit. By May we still hadn't heard what we were doing there. Then on June 1 all letter writing was stopped, and that was our first clue that something was ready to happen.

On the third of June all the troops were assembled, and it was just a mass of humanity—people loading the ships, loading trucks and tanks onto ships. It was a pretty gratifying feeling, looking at this and saying, "Holy smokes, look at all this stuff. How could we lose the war?" When we got on our ship we were told what our destination was, and there wasn't much we could do at that point but prepare ourselves. We were very well trained physically for what lay ahead. Mentally, though, each person is different. When you think you are going to face the enemy and you wonder, "How long have I got? Will I survive?" you want to be in the best shape spiritually to face your Creator.

When we finally crossed the Channel on the morning of the sixth, we had to go from the ship onto those landing crafts that would take us to the shore. There were big scramble nets that led down into the landing crafts because they were probably about twenty-five or thirty feet below the level of the ship.

Here we were with all of our gear—I don't know how we even got our legs over the side of the ship. We had a gas-resistant suit that was very cumbersome, we had our rifle belt, and we had to carry ninety-six rounds of ammunition, our canteens, our entrenching tool, our gas mask, our life jacket, our K-rations, and our rifles. I mean, we were weighed down. I had a strange, nightmarish feeling, sort of like, "Is this a dream or is this reality?" But then we lined up and they called my name and over the side I went. I don't know how we did it, but somehow we got down that net, even with the huge waves bobbing up.

Our battleships had already started firing on the beach by the time my unit got there, and it was glorious to see the big belches of orange flame coming out of our guns. Then we saw the 82nd and the 101st Airborne, and to see those darlings up there gave us a marvelous feeling. It was reassuring to think that we might have it relatively easy going in. But as we got closer to the beach we saw these big black plumes of smoke, and we knew that the German artillery had opened up and was zeroing in on the beaches where we were headed.

Then the ramp on the landing craft went down. A good buddy of mine started to cry and scream, "I can't go in, I can't." The poor guy just broke up. I said, "You gotta go, you gotta," and I grabbed him with one arm and inflated our life jackets, and threw him in the water. I jumped in and tried to help him by myself, but he was hysterical. Another one of my buddies came along and got on the other side of this guy, and I said, "We gotta go, we gotta go," because the longer we were out there the longer we were subjected to artillery fire, and we could get hit at any time.

We held our rifles over our heads and submerged ourselves in the water to protect us as much as we could. I was exhausted, weighed down, but then I got mad. I started cursing, and I told myself, "Nothing is going to stop me until I get on that beach." Fortunately, I got there, and I took off as best I could up the beach to some kind of wall, where we took cover until we could regroup.

At a time like that you don't hold out too much hope that you're going to survive this whole war. Some of us did, and some of us didn't. God rest their souls that lie over there in foreign soil.

The first units of the invasion, taking advantage of the element of surprise, made their way quickly into the farmland at Gold, Juno, and Sword beaches.

But the Americans pushing in at Omaha Beach were not so lucky. There, in the center of the front, soldiers walked into a wall of German gunfire. Attempting to scale a cliff well covered by German defenders, more than 2,000 GIs were killed or wounded. But by nightfall they had secured it and joined the 156,000 other Allied soldiers on their way to liberating France. The invasion of Normandy had been a success.

By August the Allies had freed Paris and turned east. But the Germans were not ready to give up. They mounted one last strike through Belgium in what became known as the Battle of the Bulge. Hitler was still fighting, but by early 1945 Germany was surrounded. From the east, the Russian army pushed through Poland and headed for the German capital, Berlin. Meanwhile the Allies were advancing from the west. Hitler retreated to his bunker in Berlin, hoping for a miracle. But his fate—and Germany's—was sealed. In April 1945, as Russian shells began pounding Berlin, Hitler swallowed a lethal dose of cyanide. Within days Germany surrendered.

Crowds in New York, London, Paris, and Moscow went wild with excitement. But the news from Berlin did not slow the pace of the war on the other side of the globe, in the Pacific.

When the marines landed on Saipan in 1944, within striking distance of Tokyo, they battled fiercely against Japanese soldiers, losing more than sixteen thousand men. Then they found themselves fighting wave upon wave of Japanese civilians. Fighting on Guam later that year, marines encountered desperate Japanese soldiers armed only with pitchforks, baseball bats, bottles, and rocks. On one coral-reef island after another, Americans waged war against an enemy whose will to fight never faltered. By the summer of 1945 the United States was bombing Tokyo, Osaka, Kobe, Kawasaki, and Yokohama, obliterating every military target and killing hundreds of thousands of civilians. Yet the Japanese people's devotion to Emperor Hirohito meant that Japan would fight on. Throughout the Pacific, American soldiers nervously waited for the invasion of Japan to begin, dreading another long, gruesome battle.

Only a few people knew that America was testing a secret weapon in the summer of 1945. And they never called it a bomb. The secretary of war called it "X." The scientists at the New Mexico test site called it "the gadget." But it was really the first atomic bomb, and its power to destroy was incredible.

Seventy-five crack fliers had been training for months, having volunteered for a mysterious secret assignment. All they knew was that they would be doing "something different." During practice flights, the men had been instructed to wear welder's goggles and never look back at their target. That was strange enough. But when they were told they would be dropping one bomb and only one bomb, they were really puzzled. Then they learned that this one bomb would carry the force of twenty thousand tons of dynamite.

Late on August 5, 1945, this special bomb was loaded onto Lieutenant Colonel Paul Tibbets's plane, a B-29 he had named *Enola Gay,* after his mother. At 2:45 A.M. the plane lumbered down the runway and lifted off into the darkness. Its mission was nothing less than a quick and sudden end to the Pacific war. Seven minutes after the flight began, Tibbets asked his crew if they knew what they were really carrying. "A chemist's nightmare?" asked the tail gunner. Tibbets told him to guess again. "A physicist's nightmare?" he asked. Then the truth dawned on him. "Colonel," he said, "are we splitting atoms today?"

The crew flew onward without talking much. Then, at 8:15 A.M. on August 6, the bombardier squeezed the release latch, dropping the bomb over the city of Hiroshima.

Junji Sarashina, born in 1929, was a student in Hiroshima who survived the destruction of the city.

In the summer of 1945 I was sixteen years old and a junior in high school. August 6 seemed like any other day. All my classmates and I were working in a munitions factory, as we had since we were freshmen. I had just stepped out of the factory and walked behind a two-story building when I saw this big ball of orange fire. The whole building—and the earth itself, it seemed—moved once to the left and once to the right, and then everything started to fall on top of me. I hit the ground immediately. After everything settled down, I found that I was covered with glass, boards, rocks, and sand. I walked to the nurse's office to find bandages and medications, as we had been trained to do. I broke the medicine chest open with a bat and carried some first-aid supplies to my friends.

A while later we went out into the street only to discover that the entire town of Hiroshima was ablaze. We could see the smoke of those famous mushroom clouds, and the skies were all dark. We started to walk toward the bridge, which was only about a quarter of a mile away, but we couldn't cross it because it was covered with people. They were all hurt, all burned. Some were dead. A lot of people were floating in the river; some were swimming, but some of them were dead, drifting with the current. Their skin was red and their clothes were nothing but strips of cloth hanging from them. Our teacher decided we should go back to the factory to spend the night. All night long we watched the town burn.

Early on August 7, some of us left the factory and started to go toward my high school. We walked through the town. Since the town was still burning, you had to be careful where you walked, tiptoeing to keep from stepping on people. When we got to my school, we found that about 285 out of the 300 students died. I tried to help some of the kids out of the swimming pool, but they just rolled right back in, their skin peeling right off from their arms. I walked back to the dormitory, where I stayed for about two days more. People began to fear typhoid, and they wanted to start cremating bodies. Someone had to do it, so I helped cremate some of my fellow students.

On the third day I went back to where my mom lived, in the countryside. The train was full of wounded people, dying people. When I finally made it to my house my mother couldn't believe I was still alive. I remember she hugged me so hard that I told her I couldn't breathe. The course I had taken, walking through town, trying to help people and cremating some of my friends, that was a really terrible thing. I actually took a step through hell and returned.

The crew of the *Enola Gay* had seen the atomic bomb do its terrible work. The devastation was stunning. "My God," wrote the copilot, "what have we done?"

CHAPTER 3

An Uneasy Peace

1946–1952

The end of World War II was the beginning of prosperous times in the United States. The booming wartime economy had turned the Great Depression upside down, and now the future of the nation seemed limitless. Of all the warring countries, only America came out of World War II stronger than before. Europe had been bombed and shelled into rubble. Japan had been burned by two atomic bombs (a second bomb had been dropped on the city of Nagasaki). But America in the late 1940s was a bustling, busy nation of abundance.

No problem seemed too big for American know-how and energy. American medicine unveiled the first forms of penicillin and other antibiotics, suggesting that disease was just one more enemy that Americans could lick. American scientists also built the first electronic computer. It was a thirty-ton monster with the computing power of a 1980s pocket calculator, but for its time, it was incredible. It suggested that Americans could tackle any problem, no matter how complex.

After living through the gloom and poverty of the Great Depression and giving 100 percent for the war effort, Americans felt they deserved some rest and relaxation. It was great to be home, swinging in the hammock in the sunshine, watching the kids play. And it felt great to be an American, a savior to much of the world.

Walter Girardin, born in 1919, was a GI from California who summed up the feeling of many veterans when they finally got home.

When I got discharged and sent home from Europe at the end of the war, they flew me down to Burbank, where my family was. My wife met me at the airport. She was beautiful, as usual. I just didn't want to let go of her. And that was the first time I'd seen our daughter since she was a little over a year old, and there she was, almost four. My wife told me that during the war, whenever my daughter saw a photo or a film of a man in uniform, she would say, "There's

Daddy." Coming home, it's a joyous occasion. You're filled with tears, but you're so happy.

In southern California at that time, things were booming. Jobs were plentiful, and salaries were better than they were in other parts of the country. It seemed to me that everything was moving more rapidly than it had been before I left. Cities were growing, big highways were popping up everywhere—even the cars seemed faster. I felt excited by it all, and also determined to succeed and make something of myself. Suddenly I felt very confident about my future.

I got us a Veterans Administration loan and bought a bigger house down the street. Somebody had bought up an old strawberry field, divided it up into lots, and built forty-two houses. They looked a little different on the outside, but they were all pretty much the same floor plan on the inside. I had to work overtime to help pay for it, but oh, how wonderful it was. And there was a great camaraderie between all of the young families in the neighborhood. We used to have barbecues and parties, play golf together, and our kids ran around together. In fact, when my wife was pregnant with our second daughter, I think there were ten or twelve other women in the neighborhood who were pregnant at the same time.

In the early days after the war, we used to think we were struggling, but we were really having a wonderful time. We were just doing all those kind of things that young families do, trying to make up for those years that we didn't have together, and everyone was having fun. It was a very happy time.

Owning a home was the dream of nearly every veteran returning from the war. Affordable houses were in demand. Builders all over the country began constructing low-cost suburban homes. Before the war, the American suburb had mostly been the playground of the rich. Now Americans were moving out of the cities and into small houses springing up in former cow pastures and cornfields. And they were moving out by the millions.

The suburbs promised green grass, safe streets, and an escape from the worries of the dawning atomic age. Americans had had enough drama during the war years. Now they wanted to enjoy the good life, with cookouts and Little League teams and bake sales. But this American dream was still out of reach for many people. Many suburbs were built for whites only. Black Americans returned from the war to find that little had changed while they had been off fighting for the world's freedom.

Howard "Stretch" Johnson, who was born in 1915, received two Purple Hearts for injuries suffered in World War II. He decided to do something to help black veterans.

Throughout the war I was in the 92nd Division, along with ten or twelve thousand other black troops. In Europe, the men of the 92nd were regarded as heroes. We liberated a number of Italian towns, including Lucca and Pisa, and when the Italian people saw these brown troops coming into their community, they just hailed us as conquering heroes. So when we came back to the United States, we expected to be treated as if we had made a contribution; we didn't like coming back into a Jim Crow scene. Most of the enlisted men in the 92nd were from the South, and it was ironic for them to return to a country for which they risked their lives, and they still had to go to the back of the bus, could not sit downstairs in the movie theater, and could not leave the plantation except with a pass from the owner.

A number of us got together and decided that it would be a good thing for us to form a black veterans' organization. One of the first things we took on was the issue of terminal leave pay. Each veteran was entitled to anywhere from $100 to $300 for having served in the U.S. Army. In the South, plantation owners attempted to prevent many of the returning veterans who worked on their plantations from getting into town to apply for their terminal leave pay. You see, blacks could only leave the plantation with a pass, and the passes were usually given for Saturday noon until Sunday evening; you couldn't leave the plantation during the work week. The application blanks for terminal leave pay were at the post office, which shut down at noon on Saturday, so it was impossible for a black veteran to pick up the application blank. So our group went to the War Department and got them to agree to release terminal leave pay blanks to our organization so we could distribute them through the Baptist Church, NAACP, and the Negro Elks Clubs. A number of our GIs went onto the plantations, sometimes dressed in blue overalls and things like that. It was almost an underground operation. We helped veterans throughout the South to get their terminal leave pay.

We also organized early bus boycotts and marches of veterans to county courthouses, to get their ballots to vote, because they had been denied the right to vote prior to World War II. We organized picket lines against job discrimination. All of these activities laid the basis for the civil rights movement of the late fifties and sixties. It was a direct outcome and carryover of the goals of World War II. The war was still being fought, in a sense.

Battles for black equality in America were being fought on several fronts. In 1947 Jack Roosevelt "Jackie" Robinson won an important victory. When Robinson strode to the plate for the Brooklyn Dodgers baseball team, he broke the "color barrier." The world of professional sports was suddenly integrated. A year later, President Harry S. Truman signed an executive order that officially integrated the armed services.

Sharpe James, born in 1936, went on to become mayor of Newark, New Jersey. He described how Jackie Robinson's achievement changed his life.

I was born in the South, but in 1944 we moved to 43 Emmett Street in Newark, which was a predominantly Irish American neighborhood. Being the only black kid in my crowd, I used to hear my white buddies say things like, "Let's get them blacks, run them blacks out of the neighborhood." But then they would always add, "We don't mean you, Sharpe." To them, "good blacks" were those that lived in their neighborhood and participated with them. Bad blacks were those in other neighborhood. So I was a "good black."

When you're poor, you've got to have a vehicle that you believe in, some kind of dream. And for all of us playing on that street, baseball was it. We all dreamed that someday we would grow up and be major-league players. The key to getting out of the ghetto for us kids was not to be a movie star or a football player. Baseball was our game, because we could wake up, go out on the street, and get a game going, which is something you couldn't do with basketball or football.

Before 1947 major-league baseball was white only. So here you had thousands of black kids like me playing baseball, but the ones with superior talent could never hope to get the same recognition that the white players would get. So as a black kid I knew I didn't have the same opportunities that the whites did, and that was really a frustration.

Then one day we got the news about Jackie Robinson. I remember all the folks in the black neighborhoods sitting around playing their card games and saying, "Did you hear? [Brooklyn Dodgers general manager] Branch Rickey's going to bring Jackie up to the majors." Everywhere you went, people had their newspapers out and they were talking about it. It was the talk of the black community because it gave hope and spirit to the downtrodden. Once Jackie broke the color barrier, I guess the thinking was that if you could break it in baseball, anything else in the world was possible. People said, "Here is a man of color who's going to make it."

To everyone in my neighborhood, white or black, Jackie Robinson was a hero. He was our role model. When we played baseball, suddenly everybody was saying, "I'm fast as Jackie Robinson," "I can catch like Jackie Robinson"—even the white guys would say that. Jackie was a thrill to watch because he was such a great athlete; his skill and aggressiveness changed the game of baseball.

Jackie's success started to affect my self-esteem, because my friends started to see my skills a different way. These white guys realized that my playing could really take me somewhere. But I think when they realized that a man of color had made it into the major leagues, they suddenly became aware that they had this good baseball player living in their community, that someday maybe I would make it like Jackie did.

———

Social progress now seemed to be joining economic prosperity. But even as Americans enjoyed the good life, many people realized that the United States could not turn its back on the world. In fact, as the Allied nation that had suffered the least, America, many people now felt, had a new responsibility. It would be up to the United States to reconstruct the war-torn world and defend it from a new enemy: the growing menace of Soviet Communism.

During the war, America and the Soviet Union had put aside their differences to fight a common threat. Now, with Germany beaten, all traces of friendship quickly disappeared. To the Soviets, America was acting like a new imperial power, ready to deny Russia the spoils of a war that had cost it dearly. To Americans, the Soviet Union looked like a nation of godless fanatics bent on spreading Communism to the four corners of the world, crushing freedom and democracy as they went. Mutual suspicion ran deep. But neither side wanted another war, especially one that might involve the new atomic weapons. And so the "Cold War" began.

In the negotiations that hammered out the rules of the peace, Russia was allowed to exert its influence over the countries its armies already occupied, but that "influence" quickly evolved into a demand that eastern Europe serve the will of the Soviet Union. Stalin took control of Poland, Hungary, Bulgaria, Rumania, East Germany, and Czechoslovakia.

In the words of Winston Churchill, an "Iron Curtain" now descended across Europe.

Americans feared that the rest of Europe was also in terrible danger. European cities were in chaos, their bridges broken, their roads torn. Many factories had been destroyed, and unemployment was rising. Poverty was spreading, with Europe's starving children crying for food. How long would it be before the Soviet Union tried to take control of these weak and desperate countries? Perhaps the most devastated country of all was Germany. Once the enemy, it was now Europe's most vulnerable nation.

American pilot Jack O. Bennett, born in 1914, had been a student in Berlin before the war. He was one of the first Americans to visit the German capital at the war's end.

When the war ended, because I was in the right place at the right time, I got to fly the first American airplane into Berlin. I took off from New York in a DC-4, a civilian airplane with big American flags on the side. As I circled around where I thought Berlin used to be, I couldn't find the city. There were no navigational aids. Even though I knew Berlin well, I nearly flew into the North Sea. And when I landed, I couldn't believe it. The city was nothing but a rubble pile.

The first thing we saw when we landed at Templehof Airport was a woman having a baby on top of a junk pile, right there amid the wrecked planes. Then all of a sudden the Russians started to lob rockets over our heads. I figured they had seen the American flag painted on the tail. A few of them came out onto the airstrip carrying these stubby machine guns. They tried to get me to take off and leave, but I wouldn't do it.

I tried to get a Jeep that afternoon. There were only two or three American officers in the whole town, and when I got in touch with them, they said, "Sure, we'll lend you a Jeep, but you're not going to be able to go downtown. There are no bridges anymore." I said, "Listen, I know Berlin well." So they gave me a Jeep, but I couldn't even get a thousand meters from the airport. I had no sense of orientation, no way to navigate. So I came back, and the officer laughed and said he would give me a German driver the next day.

The following day when my German driver picked me up, he said, "I've heard you were here, before the war." I said I was, and he said, "You're not going to like this." It turned out that every main thoroughfare was piled up five stories high with rubbish, wrecked tanks, and wrecked airplanes. We made our way to Pragerplatz and then walked a ways to find the street where I used to live. There was no apartment house there at all, and I sat down and had tears in my eyes. My driver had tears in his eyes as well. I said, "They'll never rebuild this city." He said, "No, they never will."

In 1947 General George Marshall, the secretary of state, proposed a plan to rescue Europe with billions of dollars of U.S. aid. There would be direct aid in the form of food, fuel, medicine, and emergency housing to help Europeans get back on their feet. But the bulk of the Marshall Plan would be spent on reconstructing industries so that Europeans could again take care of themselves. First Marshall had to convince Congress and the American people that they should give more aid to Europe. He got help when seven Cub Scouts from Maryland came to him to propose their own "Junior Marshall Plan." They wanted to raise money themselves to send to suffering European children their own age. Marshall was very moved by these generous Scouts. He declared that a new generation understood America's new responsibilities in the world.

The Marshall Plan began in June 1948. In just months Western Europe began to recover. Cases of malnutrition decreased. Factories started up again. People had heat for their homes. At the height of the plan, 150 ships a day brought tires, tractors, drilling equipment, chemicals, oil, cotton, and more to European ports. The Marshall Plan would save Europe for democracy.

Berlin was the setting for the first Cold War showdown between the United States and the Soviet Union. Because it was the capital of Germany, it was being governed by all the victorious powers: the Americans, the British, the French, and the Soviets. But the entire city was deep within Soviet-controlled East Germany. In June 1948, as the Marshall Plan began, Stalin decided to challenge the United States by blocking the road into Berlin from the west.

Stalin had gambled that America would not want to risk war over Berlin, and he was right. But President Truman took a gamble of his own. He decided to simply ignore Stalin's blockade and supply Berlin by air. It was an enormous challenge. For Berlin to survive, the United States would have to land four thousand tons of supplies every day—one planeload every three and a half minutes.

At first, only a thousand tons a day were getting through. Then the people of Berlin, using twenty thousand volunteers, built a third airport. By December, forty-five hundred tons of supplies were being flown in every day; by the spring it became eight thousand tons, then thirteen thousand. American and British pilots flew on little sleep, their planes dangerously overloaded. But they still managed to do something extra, dropping bags of candy from their planes as German children ran to greet them. By the middle of May, Stalin realized he was beaten. The blockade was over.

One of the most far-reaching consequences of the Second World War was the end it brought to the old colonial powers. All over the world new nations were emerging. At the same time that the Marshall Plan's ships were carrying their valuable cargo to Europe, Jewish refugees were making their way to the former British colony of Palestine. There the recently formed United Nations had established a new country, Israel. And in China the Communists, led by Mao Zedong, finally won their long battle for power.

The Communist victory in China stunned Americans. And when China and Russia signed a friendship treaty, it confirmed Americans' worst fears of a Communist world revolution. There was still more bad news. In September 1949 Americans discovered that the Soviet Union had exploded its first atomic bomb. Cold War tensions were growing.

In this environment of suspicion, people began to worry that Communists were infiltrating the United States. A rabid anti-Communism gripped many people across the country. Senator Joseph McCarthy of Wisconsin became the most influential anti-Communist of the time by playing on people's fears. In a speech one day in 1950 he announced that he had a list of 205 known Communists working in the State Department. In fact, there was no such list. (In later speeches he changed the number to 57, to 81, and then to 4.) But the uproar that greeted his statement was enormous. So McCarthy continued with his wild accusations. He went on to lead his supporters in a witch hunt that would last for years and ruin thousands of lives. *McCarthyism* has since entered the language as a word that describes the making of unfounded accusations against innocent people.

Liberal Hollywood came under heavy attack by McCarthy's forces. The entertainment industry created a blacklist—a list of "suspicious" people who were not allowed to work on television or in movies. Actress Lee Grant, who was born in 1927, found her name on that list.

In 1951 the first play I was ever in, *Detective Story*, was made into a film, and I got my first Academy Award nomination. Around that time, I was asked to speak at the memorial service for an actor I had been working with, who had been questioned by the House Un-American Activities Committee as a suspected Communist. I got up there and said that I felt he was hounded to death—that his constant appearances in front of the committee had contributed to his death. The next day, at an Actor's Equity meeting, somebody turned around to me and said, "Congratulations. You made it into *Red Channels*." This was a weekly periodical that listed the names of the people who were to be blacklisted. I felt the floor rush out from under me and my heart drop, and I said to myself, "That's it."

Of course there really weren't very many Communists in Hollywood. But once the anti-Communists had taken care of the real Communists, they started picking on people who had given money to certain organizations, people who had shown up at the "wrong" party, or people who voted for the "wrong" person—people who weren't even political at all, like me. And the entertainment industry buckled under the pressure.

Red Channels became the bible of the television industry. It was easy to make it in there—all you had to do was stand up at a union meeting and ask, "What are you trying to do about blacklisting?" Then somebody from the union board would write your name down, and the next day you'd be on the list. The Screen Actors Guild, run by Ronald Reagan, did the same thing. And once you were blacklisted, you were out of work unless you got up in front of the union and said, "I'm sorry that I gave money to that," or "I'm sorry I showed up at that party. I am a good American. I never meant to do it." You had to humiliate yourself in front of your peers, or maybe give some money to *Red Channels* as a way of showing that you supported their patriotic effort.

When I got the subpoena from the House Un-American Activities Committee asking me to testify against other actors, it was very frightening. They asked me lots of personal questions, things that could have put other people in jeopardy, because I knew all the other people in the union who were fighting blacklisting. And I could have hurt them if I talked. Being an informer meant placing your fellow actor, fellow friend, or fellow director in jeopardy. It meant that a person didn't work anymore. So taking that step was about the worst thing that you could do to anybody.

When I made a choice not to give names, I never really knew if the whole thing would ever end. It seemed like it might go on forever. Fighting the blacklist became my career.

Senator McCarthy was not the only anti-Communist who ruined careers and smeared reputations. There was a hysteria sweeping through the United States that sometimes became ridiculous. Schools banned the Robin Hood story for its "Communist" themes. The Cincinnati Reds baseball team even changed its name to the Red Legs so no one would get the wrong idea.

But there were also real Communist spies in America. Klaus Fuchs, one of the physicists who worked on the atomic bomb, had given information about the bomb to Soviet agents. He belonged to a spy ring that included nine other people, among them Julius and Ethel Rosenberg. The Rosenbergs were convicted of espionage and sentenced to death in 1951.

In the midst of this Communist scare, in 1950, President Truman decided to go to war in Korea, which had been divided at the end of World War II. The success of the Communists in China had people fearing a "domino effect": that one country after another would fall under Communist control. The Korean War began when Communist North Korea, with Stalin's blessing, invaded South Korea. The U.S. government, joining with other countries in the United Nations, believed that it had to support South Korea, especially when Chinese Communists joined the North Koreans. American forces entered the fight, and three years passed before the war ended. Korea was left ravaged. But it was still divided politically, much as it had been when the war started. Nobody really won. Nobody really lost—except the fifty-four thousand Americans and other

Allied soldiers and more than two million Koreans and Chinese who died in the fighting.

Len Maffioli, who was born in 1925, fought in the Korean War and was taken prisoner by the Chinese. He described the Chinese attempts to convert American prisoners to their cause.

On the twenty-eighth of November 1950, I was in a convoy in the Chosin Reservoir that was completely surrounded by Chinese troops. We fought them off for twelve hours, but we had an awful lot of dead and dying in the ditches, so we eventually had to surrender. We had heard about the North Koreans, that they were just as apt to execute a prisoner as they were to imprison him. But the Chinese fighting with them were different. They had the idea that they were going to put us through a political indoctrination course—what some people called a low-power brainwashing course—and actually convert us to their cause.

On December 24 they threw us a Christmas party. They had actually gone and cut down a pine tree and decorated it with pieces of colored paper. They handed each of us a few pieces of candy, five or six salted peanuts, and a tailor-made cigarette—these were our Christmas presents. And then they started this bit where they wanted us to get up and make confessions. This was a big deal in Communist brainwashing, to confess your sins.

After about a week or two, they started giving us English editions of Chinese newspapers, with certain articles circled in red. We had to read these articles and make sure we understood them, because later the Chinese would test us on them. And they were so ridiculous—stuff about Chinese soldiers who jumped on the back of an American tank, ripped open the hatch with bayonets, and threw grenades down there and killed the crew, and you were supposed to believe it. There were also stories about the terrible situation that we had in the United States. I remember one about how people were dying of starvation on the streets of Bakersfield, California. Of course, we knew all this was rot, but when we told them so, we had to listen to long-winded lectures in a barn, which meant three or four hours of freezing to death. So eventually we got the idea. They never interrogated us much on military matters; what they were more interested in was our family life, our social life. They couldn't believe that a lot of the people captured, me included, owned our own automobiles. I remember one of them saying one morning that in China he could have an egg every morning for breakfast if he wanted. And somebody laughed and said, "God, we could have a dozen if we wanted, every morning." Well, he refused to believe that food was so plentiful.

One day they called out the names of nineteen of us. They drove us in a truck and we had no idea where we were, but we could hear the sound of Allied artillery. Our Chinese guards took off in fear, and, surprisingly, some Korean civilians helped us hide out in a house. We couldn't figure out why these Koreans were helping us. Then we asked where we were and found out that we were in South Korea. That's why the Koreans were so friendly.

We were just overjoyed to be back with the Allies. We were the only group ever to escape from the enemy in Korea. And we were the first Allied troops to come home as graduates of the political indoctrination course.

The conflict in Korea left many people in the United States confused. If it was a war worth fighting in the first place, why wasn't it worth fighting to a real victory? General Douglas MacArthur, the commander of the American forces in Korea, agreed. He had driven the Communists out of South Korea, and he'd wanted to go further, to push his troops through North Korea and into mainland China. But President Truman had ordered MacArthur to turn back. He was afraid that any move directly against the Chinese could trigger a nuclear war.

The Korean War was America's first limited war. Though it frustrated many Americans not to fight on to a real victory, the terrifying specter of nuclear weapons demanded caution. No one wanted to risk starting World War III—because now that both the United States and the Communists had nuclear weapons, fighting an all-out war could mean the end of the world.

CHAPTER 4

Mass Markets

1953–1961

America was transformed in the 1950s. Home life changed as people left farms and cities for the suburbs. Work life changed, with more people now employed at desk jobs and in stores than on farms and in factories. Shopping changed, making room for new chain stores and the first suburban malls. Supermarkets began to replace grocery stores, McDonald's started to push out the old-fashioned roadside diners, and Holiday Inns were forcing downtown hotels to shut their doors. The American economy was booming, and more people than ever before shared in the good life.

Many Americans were enjoying the fruits of success for the first time: health insurance, vacations, savings accounts, their own homes. They flocked to the suburbs to find a new way of life. But leaving hometowns behind often meant losing connections to ethnic traditions and family support systems. In an attempt to create new ties, these people tried hard to blend in, to be just like their neighbors. They wanted to create a place where they felt comfortable, part of a community. The promise of suburbia was safety and newness. If the price was, for some, a loss of individuality, well, was that really so important? Wasn't it better to be a team player, to put up a united front—especially to show the Soviets that the American way of life was a superior one? It felt almost like a patriotic duty to show your team spirit.

Harriet Osborn was born in 1928. Her experience of moving to a brand-new suburb was typical for many families.

Moving into the suburbs was an adventure. We traveled twelve hours from Boston with a truckload of furniture. I sat in the front with the goldfish, the plants, and my son on my lap. We lived too far away to prepare our new home before our arrival. In fact, we hadn't even seen the house. We arrived and took our first steps through the back door and into our new home. I remember it took me five hours to get from my back door to the bedrooms because of the parade of salesmen waiting to greet us on our arrival. They were selling landscaping, storm windows, and milk and bread and diapers. It was really something. One day after we were all moved in, the property was landscaped.

One of the most important things about suburban life was forming a bond with your neighbors. Our town was a veritable melting pot, with people coming from all over upstate Pennsylvania, New Jersey, and Philadelphia. I think we confided in each other to alleviate the loneliness of coming from different sections of the country. Mothers and dads and grandparents weren't there. Sisters and brothers weren't there. We shared the same problems of trying to build a home, raise children, and find work. Everybody was the same age, and everybody wore the same clothes.

The woman's role was to keep the home fires burning. We were expected to keep a clean home, to look after and discipline our children, and to take care of our husbands. It was very easy, really, yet we were all a bit lonesome. There were many, many get-togethers. Around ten o'clock in the morning we'd sit out and have coffee klatches, and there'd be kids running all around and you'd be watching this child and that child.

The suburbs were the perfect place to

raise children, and children were our primary focus. The statistics said that every home had at least two and a half children. When we first moved to our town there were only three obstetricians. As the birthrate rose, the obstetricians extended their office hours to 2:00 A.M. Many times in the newspaper we'd see at least three columns of names listed in the birth announcements for the week. There was much emphasis placed on babies and bringing them up during their first year of life. Once in a while we'd hear a seminar on how to raise children. Everything in the stores was geared toward children. It was always, "What do children want and what will parents buy for their children?"

The television also served as a baby-sitter. You could just put your children in front of the TV, and while they watched *Davy Crockett* and *Ding Dong School,* you could make supper. TV was our information box and our link to the outside world, and, of course, it entertained us. My family always loved the dramas and the variety and comedy shows. We saw Elvis on *The Ed Sullivan Show.* We loved the programs that focused on family, like *Ozzie and Harriet* and *Leave It to Beaver.* We identified with these pictures on the television screen, and they became an integral part of our lives.

Television had arrived shortly after World War II. Many people regarded it as a miracle, a miniature theater right in their own homes. Americans had bought more than forty-five million television sets by the end of the 1950s, and they were spending a third of their waking hours watching television.

More often than not, TV programs conformed to the same family values that people looked for in the suburbs. Old radio shows that had ethnic or working-class characters didn't make the transition to television. New shows such as *Father Knows Best* and *Ozzie and Harriet* showed Americans what they wanted to see in themselves: a complete family with a working father, an aproned mother, and cheerful, friendly children living in a comfortable home. Comedy changed, too. Because television was visual, it was perfect for sight gags and goofy slapstick. Variety shows with a mix of comic sketches and pop music were the rage.

Sid Caesar, born in 1922, was the star of *Your Show of Shows,* one of the most popular programs of the 1950s.

In the 1950s I think people liked television so much because it was about them. They would see things on television that would remind them of events in their own life. That was the key to the success of *Your Show of Shows*: We always wrote sketches about things that happened to normal people. Quite often it was drawn directly from things that happened to us. When we would write a sketch, the most important thing was how does this affect the people—the people that have to wait in line, that have to park the car. Writing for television, you had the feeling that you were communicating with the people.

Most of the time we had little choice but to write from our own experiences. We had an hour-and-a-half-long show to write every week. So we needed new ideas, as well as things we could always go back to. If we did a certain kind of sketch—like a husband-and-wife sketch—and it went well, then we'd do another husband-and-wife sketch. If we did a satire of a movie, we'd say, "Hey, we can do more movie satires." One time, the writers and I went into a delicatessen for lunch and it was so crowded you couldn't move. They seated us at this table by a swinging door that led to the kitchen. So I'm sitting there eating my sandwich and bang—the door keeps flying open and hitting me on the back. The next week we wrote a sketch about that very same thing. There's this guy who gets seated next to a kitchen door, and every time the waiter tries to serve him, the door comes flying open and he gets smashed all around. So, in taking our sketches from things that happened to us firsthand, we hoped we were giving the audience something they could see themselves in and laugh at.

One of the things that separated television from radio was that people had to sit still to watch it. Before television, people could do chores or housework or eat meals while the radio played in the background. But television required people to change their behavior to fit the program schedule. Studies showed an increase in toilet flushing when the most popular shows broke for commercials. The Swanson food company realized that television was interrupting the family meal. In 1954 Swanson created the first TV Dinner, a frozen meal packaged in a little foil tray that could be rushed from the oven to the living room and eaten in front of the television set.

The advertisements on television helped reinforce a uniform American culture. For the first time products could actually be seen, not just described, to millions of customers all over the country. Television commercials began to create the desire for products that Americans hadn't even known about.

Maxwell Dane, born in 1906, founded an advertising firm that quickly recognized the power of television for selling new consumer products.

When we first started the company, we relied primarily on print advertising with some radio sprinkled in. Then as the fifties wore on, television came into its own and really changed things. Suddenly you had this visual medium where you could reach millions of people—coast to coast—all at one time. And you could control exactly what the people would see and what they would hear. It was a very powerful medium. No advertising agency could ignore television. One of our earliest and most successful major television campaigns was for the Polaroid Land camera, which took pictures that developed instantly. Of course, live television was the perfect medium to show off the virtues of an instant camera. The viewers actually got to see the picture develop before their eyes. Since it was live television, we had no control when things went wrong. Once one of our spokesmen, I think it was Steve Allen, took a picture that didn't develop properly. Being the professional that he was, he just simply took another photograph and said, "See? You know instantly whether or not you've got the shot."

In addition to handling American companies overseas, we also acquired a few foreign clients—Volkswagen being our most famous. When we first landed the Volkswagen account in the early fifties, they were selling very few cars in America. This was the era of the big American car. The Volkswagen was unique in its smaller size, lower cost, and low fuel consumption. It was a simple, reliable, and very unusual car, so [my partner] Bill Bernbach developed an advertising campaign that reflected that. His ads stressed the quality and reliability of the car and were aimed at people looking for an affordable second car, as well as the growing youth market looking to buy its first car.

The growing youth market began to drive cultural change in America. After World War II the baby boom brought an enormous number of children into the world. These children, together with teenagers, created a huge youth population. Even the term *teenager* was only first used widely in the 1940s. In the years before World War I, children usually finished school by the age of fifteen and went to work. The expansion of secondary education in the 1920s and, now, the prosperity of the 1950s allowed childhood to last longer. Children enjoyed their parents' higher standard of living as well. With bigger allowances and more leisure time, they became consumers, too.

Television eagerly grabbed hold of this huge audience. *American Bandstand* was a wildly popular television dance show, introducing new music, dance styles, and fashions to children who watched at home. The younger crowd wanted to shake things up, and music was one way they were going to do it. At the same time, shows such as *American Bandstand* helped make popular culture even more uniform, with teens around the country dressing alike and dancing alike to the same tunes.

Bunny Gibson, who was born in 1946, was one of the teenage dancers on *American Bandstand*.

American Bandstand was kind of like the first televised revolution of teenagers in this country. We could watch the show and see our peers dance, and then we could go out and buy records of the music that we heard. That show brought all the teenagers together. It's the first time that we could identify with other teenagers that were on TV. When I was growing up in Darby, Pennsylvania, I would run home from Catholic school every day to watch *American Bandstand*. I couldn't wait to turn on the TV. When I watched the show, I felt liberated. It made me forget about my problems at Catholic school and the difficult life I had at home. I would watch the kids on the show dance, and I would dance along. I would spin around and do all the steps using the banister or the refrigerator door as a partner. I got pretty good with that old banister. I figured if I could dance that well alone, imagine how I would be with a real partner. So I decided to go down and try and get on that show.

One day I stole fifty cents from my mother's purse, played hooky from school, and hopped on a bus downtown. I tried to look older by putting on lots of makeup. You see, I was only thirteen, and the minimum age for *Bandstand* was fourteen. I was so nervous while waiting in line to get in. I was sure somebody was going to tap me on the shoulder and say that I was too young. But the minute I walked through those green doors, I knew I was at home. And that little studio became my home for the next several years. It was really the first place where I felt like I belonged.

Even on *Bandstand* we had to conform. We had a strict dress code. The guys all had crew cuts and wore ties and jackets. All of the girls' dresses had to come up high on the neck and could not reveal too much. I think that really helped change the image of rock and roll. How could rock and roll be the devil's music when all of the kids on *Bandstand* looked so nice and clean? I think the show really helped to smooth over the image of rock and roll and to bring it into the mainstream.

In the fifties we were supposed to listen to our parents and not really have a lot of thoughts of our own. We were supposed to do what we were told, which didn't really allow for much freedom. But like me, a lot of teenagers wanted to be able to find things out for ourselves: who we were inside, what we liked, what we wanted to do. Rock and roll was music from the heart and the soul that gave us a feeling of freedom. And once we got that freedom, it was like the parents really lost their control over us.

Rock and roll was the music of a new generation. To many parents, it seemed like a revolution. The most famous rock-and-roll revolutionary was Elvis Presley. Elvis's songs seemed innocent enough, with silly lyrics about "hound dogs" and "blue suede shoes." But his music and his performance style were something else entirely. The roots of Elvis's rock and roll were in the rhythm-and-blues music of America's black community. But Elvis added a country-and-western beat. Onstage, he curled his lip and swung his hips, and teenage girls swooned. Boys copied his "ducktail" hairdo. America's white teenagers found their role model in Elvis and made rock and roll their music.

Sam Phillips, born in 1923, founded Sun Records, where Elvis first recorded.

In the early 1950s rhythm and blues was considered the music of black people. It was even called "race music," which meant that it was black music played by and for black folks. At Sun Records, I recorded primarily black rhythm-and-blues artists. And in talking to friends at radio stations across the country, it was evident that a lot of white kids were listening to black rhythm and blues. A lot of the adults I talked to were worried about that. I would always just look them straight in the eye and tell them, "Your kids aren't falling in love with black or white or green or yeller. They're falling in love with the vitality of the music."

From very early on, the biggest thing that I hoped to achieve was to find a white person who could help broaden the base of rhythm-and-blues music and to help us get over this black and white thing. To me, Elvis Presley was the perfect person to take black rhythm and blues and combine it with white country blues into something interesting. Now, I was criticized plenty by people saying, "Hey, man, you have been recording our black artists, and now you're going to steal it and give it to some white kid." But I never set out to steal anything. I just wanted this exciting music to be heard by the widest audience possible.

When I sent a copy of Elvis's first record to the editor of *Billboard* magazine, he said that I had to either be a fool or a genius to have Elvis sing a blues song on one side ("That's All Right, Mama") and a country bluegrass anthem ("Blue Moon of Kentucky") on the back side. Nobody had ever combined a black rhythm-and-blues song with a white country hit; you just didn't mix things up like that. Also, Elvis's versions of these songs were unlike anything ever done before; they were fast, exciting, and powerful.

When "That's All Right, Mama" and "Blue Moon of Kentucky" turned the corner and became hits, that was the defining moment when people began to feel the music and not think about whether it's black or white. Once word got around about what was happening with Elvis, it opened the doors for a lot of other singers, and it ultimately helped change the way people felt about music and about race.

On December 1, 1955, after a long day at work, a forty-two-year-old seamstress named Rosa Parks boarded a bus in Montgomery, Alabama, for her ride home. Montgomery, like most southern cities, operated a segregated bus system—the front rows of seats were for white riders, the back rows for black riders. Being a "Negro," Parks took her place at the front of the black section. But when the bus reached the next stop, enough whites got on to fill the seats at the front, leaving one white man standing. The bus driver told Parks and three other black riders to give up their seats. The three others moved, but Parks remained where she was. The driver warned that he would have her arrested, but Rosa Parks stayed calm and stayed put.

Rosa Parks's arrest set off a chain of events that could not be stopped. Within hours a well-organized network of civil rights leaders in Montgomery had decided to organize a boycott of the bus system. It was the perfect opportunity to challenge the constitutionality of the city's segregation laws. To lead the effort, the black community chose a young minister named Martin Luther King Jr.

King's strategy was one of passive resistance. He called it "Christianity in action." He told his followers to commit no violence, no matter how strongly they were provoked. "Blood may flow . . . before we receive our freedom," he said, "but it must be our blood." To keep the boycott going, more than twenty thousand black citizens formed car pools, rode bicycles, hired taxis, or walked to work. By saying no, Rosa Parks had triggered one of the most dramatic demonstrations of nonviolent protest in American history.

The Montgomery bus boycott lasted more than a year, and Inez Jessie Baskin, born in 1916, was part of it.

I took the bus to work every day. Our bus system was segregated, just like practically everything else. There was no specific line of demarcation separating seats reserved for white and black passengers. It was usually at the bus driver's discretion, and it varied depending on the time of day and the driver, but you were just supposed to know. One thing was for certain: When a white person occupied a seat, even if it was one man to an entire long seat, blacks had to walk right on past. About six o'clock one evening I received a phone call from a friend's mother telling me to go to the Dexter Avenue Church. That's where I heard about Rosa Parks's arrest. I had first met Rosa Parks during the time that I was a member of the NAACP. She had always impressed me. She was just an angel walking. When I arrived, a small group of people were gathered in the church basement, and they were already talking about boycotting the local bus system and spreading some leaflets around about it.

News of the boycott spread pretty quickly. The telephones were ringing off the wall all over town. I was wondering how many people were going to get on the bus in the morning, because some of us had to travel five or six miles to get to work. But when Monday morning came, there were empty buses wherever you looked. That night a mass meeting was held at the Holt Street Baptist Church. It was not a large church, but it was packed to the rafters with people from all walks of life. We were all waiting for Dr. King, who had just been chosen as our spokesperson. There were people singing the Negro spirituals. You just don't need an organ and a cathedral the size of St. Peter's when a thousand black voices are singing with all their feelings and pathos. Everything was coming out in these songs. Dr. King finally arrived and came in through the side door while everyone was singing. There was first a hush, and then the whole place exploded. Martin Luther King spoke in a very soft, rich voice, and as he was going along, you'd get the feeling that this was not just something on paper, but rather that here was a person who really cared.

I remember one particular day during the boycott when everyone was asked to walk to wherever you had to go. From where I lived to my office was approximately eight miles, and it was drizzling and it was cold. As we walked we just kept conversing and singing, but by the time I was halfway to work, the singing and conversation weren't helping me very much because I was damp and cold. But then I heard that an older woman had said, "My feets is tired, but my soul is resting." There were plenty of elderly persons walking with us, and when you saw them walking, singing, and smiling, you knew you just had to go on. I thought, "If they can do it, so can I."

The night the boycott ended, I was thinking about getting a little sleep when the telephone rang. It was a friend saying, "Get up. I'm picking you up. The buses are running." Well, that opened my eyes. We went right over to the bus stop in front of Dr. King's house on Jackson Street, just as the bus pulled up. I got out of the car and waltzed up to the bus. I stepped onto the bus, and the bus driver held out his hand for the bus fare. I didn't have a dime in my pocket. Fortunately, one of the ministers gave me bus fare, and so I got on the bus with Dr. King and Dr. Abernathy, right up in front.

I had been living in Montgomery most of my life, and up until then, you couldn't even get three people to stay together for two hours. And here we had all come together as one for 381 days. It made me feel that there was more to this cohesiveness. There was more than Dr. Martin Luther King and Rosa Parks involved in this. It was Providence. I still believe that.

The bus boycott and other civil rights protests throughout the South were covered on national television. On television, the issue of civil rights was made plain and simple through the power of images. While the nation watched, peaceful demonstrators asking for the most basic equality and respect were blasted with water from fire hoses and attacked with police dogs.

Some of the most frightening civil rights clashes were over integrating American schools. In 1954 the Supreme Court had ruled that whites-only schools were illegal. Three years later nine black students were chosen to integrate Central High School in Little Rock, Arkansas. The governor of Arkansas, Orval Faubus, opposed integration. He sent the Arkansas National Guard to turn away the black students when they came to school. The mayor of Little Rock, fearing violence, asked Washington for help. President Eisenhower sent troops to Little Rock to restore the peace and make sure the black students were allowed to go to school.

Anne Thompson, born in 1942, was a student at Central High when integration first came to the schools.

I was a fifteen-year-old tenth grader when they made the announcement that they were going to integrate Little Rock Central High. At first many of the parents refused to believe that it was actually going to happen. Some parents formed groups and committees to try and stop it.

The day the black students arrived, there was a circuslike atmosphere around the school. There was fear and there was anger, but there was a lot of excitement, too. It was almost as if something fun was about to happen. There were all of the cameras and reporters, and all of the parents were there, urging us on and telling us to go out there and not let them in. The parents gathered in this vacant lot directly across the street from the school. There was so much electricity and tension coming from that vacant lot that something big was bound to happen. Every now and then fights would break out among the parents. There were things said and done over there that frightened me much more than these black students did.

At one point an elderly black man in a blue and white Chevrolet drove up Fourteenth Street alongside Central High School. Suddenly all of these white parents surrounded the car and started yelling. I was so afraid they were going to turn that car over with the elderly black man in it. I honestly believe that had the parents stayed away, there wouldn't have been a problem. The whole thing was at their insistence. We were all thinking, "Well, we're just doing what our parents want us to do." We almost felt like we didn't have a choice; we had to get out there and protest.

Many white Americans were sympathetic to the black struggle. For years now, they had been displaying the American democratic dream before the world, especially the Soviet Union. But here in their own country many Americans were being treated as second-class citizens, simply because they were black. Americans were beginning to examine their national values with a critical eye.

A new challenge to American complacency became visible in the sky on October 5, 1957. The first satellite ever launched was orbiting the earth. The trouble was that this satellite had been launched not by America but by the Soviet Union. The Russians had beaten the Americans into space.

This news was hard for Americans to accept. They had always believed that democracy's free exchange of ideas would keep American science ahead of Soviet science. For Russians, the launch of *Sputnik* (Russian for "fellow traveler") was a major achievement, signaling their importance on the world stage.

Semyon Reznik, born in 1938, was a Russian student in Moscow when *Sputnik* was launched. He shared his country's excitement.

One of the reasons that scientific progress took on such importance during those years was our belief that through technological progress, the Soviet Union would be victorious over the United States. I myself loved science and believed in scientific progress, because it would move history forward faster, just as the Marxists claimed it would. Science and technology would make our production more efficient, making life easier for us, the workers. I thought science would make our society better in a moral sense and a social sense. So I was very excited about the fact that the Soviet space program was advancing so rapidly.

The day our satellite *Sputnik* was launched, a special voice came over the radio to announce it to us. Traditionally in the Soviet Union a few of the radio announcers were hired to read only the most urgent news on the radio. We always knew when something extra special was coming over the airwaves, as we would hear a special signal, *ta ta toe, ta toe, ta toe,* and then one of those readers with a deep voice would begin speaking. And if your radio wasn't on at home, a neighbor would let you know immediately.

On an October morning in 1957 we heard one of those voices announce, "Attention. All radio stations of the Soviet Union are broadcasting. . . . Our satellite *Sputnik* is in space." I felt so proud. Who did it? We did it! The Soviet Union is first in space!

There was a growing uneasiness in America in the late 1950s. Perhaps it came from the moral challenge of the civil rights movement. Perhaps it came from the technological challenge of the space race. People felt that a new, more difficult era was coming, and they looked for a new leader to inspire them. In 1960 television brought the presidential candidates before an audience of millions, and the handsome young Senator John Fitzgerald Kennedy of Massachusetts shone. He was confident, energetic, and ambitious, and he had lofty goals. His message was just what the youthful American culture wanted to hear: Let's all work together to make this nation worthy of its high ideals. Kennedy electrified America's youth.

Journalist Jeff Greenfield, born in 1943, was inspired by presidential candidate John Kennedy.

If you were a teenager in the 1950s, the president, Dwight Eisenhower, looked a lot like your grandfather. In fact, he was old enough to be your grandfather—the oldest man ever to have served as president at that time. By the late fifties he'd been through a heart attack and a stroke, and he was never particularly good with the English language. To my parents' generation, he was the guy who won World War II. But to my generation, he just looked like a somewhat befuddled elderly gentleman.

So along comes this 1960 campaign and John Kennedy. The idea that this guy, who looked like your cool older brother, might be president of the United States was a really exciting proposition. Kennedy came to my college, the University of Wisconsin, and I had a seat several miles high up in the bleachers. There was this impossibly tanned, impossibly energetic young guy giving a rousing speech about our generation and what it meant. And it connected, because we were not cynics then. It was possible to listen to somebody running for president of the United States talk about our responsibilities as the next generation, and believe it.

I watched all the debates in the common rooms on campus, and they were absolutely packed. I think we all felt a sense of identification, and it wasn't just that he was young. Kennedy seemed to suggest that there was some role for us in the world.

The idea of a White House run and staffed by younger people suggested that government and politics were not simply the province of people impossibly older than we were. There was the feeling that, well, if they're running the political system, surely we can be somehow involved in it. It gave us a sense that we were entitled to be part of the political process, even as naysayers and protesters. Because, after all, look who was running the country.

On November 8, 1960, John Fitzgerald Kennedy was elected the thirty-fifth president of the United States. With Martin Luther King, he shared the flame of idealism. President Kennedy, or JFK, as he was known, gave one of the most persuasive inaugural addresses in history. It was short, poetic, and inspiring. The torch had been passed to a new generation, he declared. Then he called on all Americans to live up to their ideals. "Ask not what your country can do for you," he said, "ask what you can do for your country." JFK challenged Americans to look deep into their consciences and create a better nation.

INDEX

A

advertising, 89–91
African Americans
  discrimination against, 63,
    64–68, 97–103
  labor unions and, 5
  music and, 94–96
  veteran rights and, 64–66
  See also civil rights
    movement
American Bandstand, 92–
    94
Anschluss, 8–9
antibiotics, 60–61
atomic bomb, 56–59, 60,
    69, 74, 78
Auschwitz, 46–49
Austria, German invasion
    of, 3, 8–11
Axis alliance, 27

B

baby boom, 91–92
baseball, 66–68
Baskin, Inez Jessie, 98–101
Bennett, Jack O., 70–72
Berlin, blockade of, 70–74
Black, Sheila, 28–31

C

Caesar, Sid, 87–89
China, 1, 74, 78–81, 82
Churchill, Winston, 23, 27,
    70
civil rights movement, 65–
    66, 97–103, 105
Cold War, 69–70, 73, 74
  See also Communism;
    space race
colonialism, end of, 74
Communism, 69, 74–82
  See also Cold War
computer, 61
Curtis, Earle, 42–44
Czechoslovakia, 1, 3, 18, 69

D

Dane, Maxwell, 90–91
D-Day, 50–55
democracy, 22, 69, 73, 103–
    104
Dunkirk, battle of, 23–27

E

Eisenhower, Dwight D., 39,
    50–51, 102, 106
Enola Gay, 57, 59

F

Faubus, Orval, 101
Four Freedoms, 35
Franco, Francisco, 1, 7
Fuchs, Klaus, 78

G

Galdonik, Clair, 51–54
Germany. *See* Hitler, Adolf;
    Nazism
Gibson, Bunny, 92–94
Giordano, Ralph, 12–13
Girardin, Walter, 61–63
Grant, Lee, 75–77
Great Depression, 1, 4, 13,
    14, 16, 21, 61
    World War II as end of,
    34, 60
Greenfield, Jeff, 106–107
Guernica, 7–8

H

Hirohito, Emperor, 56
Hiroshima, 57–59
Hitler, Adolf, 1, 3, 8–9, 16,
    17, 20, 23, 27, 31,
    34, 44, 45, 49–50,
    55
Holocaust, 45–49

I

immigration, by Jews before
    World War II, 13
Iron Curtain, 70
isolationism, 4, 13, 20–22,
    31
Israel, 74

J

James, Sharpe, 66–68
Japan, 1, 27, 31, 32–36, 41,
    55–60
Jews, 8–13, 17, 20, 45–49,
    74
Johnson, Howard "Stretch,"
    64–66

K

Kennedy, John Fitzgerald
    (JFK), 105–108
King, Martin Luther, Jr.,
    97–101, 107
Korean War, 78–82
Kristallnacht, 11–13, 22
Kulski, Julian, 19–20

L

labor unions, 4–7
London blitz, 28–31

M

MacArthur, Douglas, 81–
    82
Maffioli, Len, 79–81
Maginot Line, 23
Mao Zedong, 74
Marshall, George, 72
Marshall Plan, 72–73,
    74
McCarthy, Joseph, 74–75,
    77
Michel, Ernest, 46–49
Montgomery bus boycott,
    97–101
Mussolini, Benito, 1, 27

N

National Labor Relations
Act, 4
Nazism, 8–13, 14

O

Osborn, Harriet, 84–86

P

Parks, Rosa, 97–98, 101
Pearl Harbor, 32, 34–35,
36
Pechel, Peter, 17–19
Phillips, Sam, 95–96
Poland, German invasion of,
16–20
Presley, Elvis, 86, 94–96

R

radio, 2–4, 9, 21, 36, 51,
89, 90, 95, 105
Reagan, Ronald, 76
Reuther, Victor, 4–7
Reznik, Semyon, 104–105
Robinson, Jackie, 66–68
rock and roll, 92–96
Rogalin, Paule, 24–27
Roosevelt, Franklin
Delano (FDR), 1, 22,
23, 31, 32, 35, 50,
51
Rosenberg, Julius and Ethel,
78
Russia
German invasion of, 44–
45
See also Cold War

S

Sarashina, Junji, 57–59
schools, integration of, 101–
103
segregation, 97–103
Shine, Neil, 36–40
Snow, Gilda, 14–16
space race, 103–105
Spanish Civil War, 1–3, 7–8
Sputnik, 103–105
Stalin, Joseph, 16, 31, 69,
73–74, 78
Stept, Karla, 8–11
Stuart, Bob, 21–22
suburbs, 62–63, 83–86
Swanson TV Dinner, 89

T

teenagers, 91–94
television, 14, 15, 86–94,
101, 105
Thompson, Anne, 102–103
Tibbets, Paul, 57
Trout, Bob, 2–4
Truman, Harry S., 66, 73,
78, 82

U

United Nations, 74, 78

W

Wagner, Robert, 13
women, work during
wartime, 34, 36, 39
World's Fair, 14–16
World War I, 17, 21, 22, 28,
35, 36, 40–41, 91

World War II, 1–4, 7–66,
 74, 78, 87, 91, 106
 beginning of, 16, 19
 casualties of, 41
 end of, 49–59, 60
 escalation of, 33–34

modern weaponry of,
 40–41
 See also isolationism

Y

Your Show of Shows, 87–89